20 FUN FACTS ABOUT THE COLOSSEUM

By Drew Nelson

Gareth Stevens
Publishing

Please visit our website, www.garethstevens.com. For a free color catalog of all our high-quality books, call toll free 1-800-542-2595 or fax 1-877-542-2596.

Library of Congress Cataloging-in-Publication Data

Nelson, Drew.
20 fun facts about the Colosseum / by Drew Nelson.
 p. cm. — (Fun fact file: world wonders!)
Includes index.
ISBN 978-1-4824-0465-4 (pbk.)
ISBN 978-1-4824-0466-1 (6-pack)
ISBN 978-1-4824-0462-3 (library binding)
1. Colosseum (Rome, Italy) — Juvenile literature. 2. Amphitheaters — Rome — Juvenile literature. 3. Rome (Italy) — Antiquities — Juvenile literature. 4. Rome (Italy) — Buildings, structures, etc. — Juvenile literature. I. Nelson, Drew, 1986- II. Title.
DG68.1 N45 2014
937.6—dc23

First Edition

Published in 2014 by
Gareth Stevens Publishing
111 East 14th Street, Suite 349
New York, NY 10003

Copyright © 2014 Gareth Stevens Publishing

Designer: Sarah Liddell
Editor: Greg Roza

Photo credits: Cover, p. 1 Hedda Gjerpen/E+/Getty Images; p. 5 Bryan Surgener/Shutterstock.com; pp. 6, 17 DEA/G. DAGLI ORTI/Contributor/De Agostini/Getty Images; p. 7 r. nagy/Shutterstock.com; p. 8 Lonely Planet/Lonely Planet Images/Getty Images; pp. 9, 22 DEA PICTURE LIBRARY/De Agostini Picture Library/Getty Images; p. 10 Mandadori Portfolio/UIG/Universal Images Group/Getty Images; p. 11 Photo Works/Shutterstock.com; p. 12 Duncan Walker/E+/Getty Images; p. 13 Morphart Creation/Shutterstock.com; p. 14 photo courtesy of Wikimedia Commons, Ave Caesar Morituri te Salutant.jpg; pp. 15, 16, 21 Time & Life Pictures/Contributor/Time & Life Pictures/Getty Images; p. 18 Iakov/Kalinin/Shutterstock.com; p. 19 Dorling Kindersley/Dorling Kindersley/Getty Images; p. 20 photo courtesy of Wikimedia Commons, Colosseum-exterior-2007.JPG; p. 23 photo courtesy of Wikimedia Commons, Thomas Interior of the Colosseum Rome 1832.jpg; p. 24 photo courtesy of Wikimedia Commons, Colosseum and Meta Sudans, Rome, Italy, 1890s.jpg; p. 25 photo courtesy of Wikimedia Commons, Joseph Wright of Derby The Coliseum, Rome by Daylight 1789.jpg; p. 26 WDG Photo/Shutterstock.com; p. 27 Giorgio Cosulich/Stringer/Getty Images News/Getty Images; p. 29 Petronilo G. Dangoy Jr./Shutterstock.com.

Printed in the United States of America

CPSIA compliance information: Batch #CW14GS: For further information contact Gareth Stevens, New York, New York at 1-800-542-2595.

Contents

The World Wonder. 4

Rome Wasn't Built in a Day 6

By Any Other Name. 8

Sold Out. 10

The Greatest Show on Earth 12

Taking Its Toll 16

Bigger and Better 18

Inventive Architects 20

Reduce, Reuse, Recycle 22

Fall and Rise 24

Rebirth 26

Still Standing 28

Glossary. 30

For More Information 31

Index 32

Words in the glossary appear in **bold** type the first time they are used in the text.

The World Wonder

When we think of **stadiums**, we think of Madison Square Garden in New York, Fenway Park in Boston, or the Rose Bowl in California. They're places where huge groups of people can have fun watching sports or shows.

In ancient times, people visited **amphitheaters** the same way we visit stadiums. They wanted to be entertained. The most famous amphitheater in the world is the Colosseum in Rome, Italy. This giant building was built during the Roman Empire.

Although it may not look like it now, the Colosseum was once the site of fights, hunts, and many other events.

FACT 1

It took the Romans just 9 years to build the Colosseum.

It can take longer than that to build a stadium now! Work was started on the Colosseum in AD 72, and it was completed in AD 80. It was started by Emperor Vespasian, but it was actually finished by the next emperor, Titus.

Titus

Vespasian

Titus was the son of Vespasian. Together, they were both members of the Flavian dynasty, or ruling family.

The Colosseum was last used during the Roman Empire in the 6th century. Today, it's a popular tourist location.

FACT 2

The Colosseum has stood for almost 2,000 years.

The Colosseum was used for shows and sporting events for about 500 years. However, this giant building has been an important location at the center of Rome for almost 2,000 years.

7

FACT 3

The building's real name isn't the "Colosseum."

The Colosseum's actual name is the Flavian Amphitheater. "Flavian" was the family name of emperors Vespasian and Titus. "Colosseum" is a nickname given to the building by ancient Romans. It comes from the Latin word *colossus*—a term used to describe very large **statues**.

AMPHITHEATRVM · FLAVIVM
TRIVMPH S · SPECTACVLISQ · INSIGNE
DIIS · GENTIVM · IMP O · CVLTV · DICATVM
MARTYRVM · CRVORE · AB · IMPVRA · SVPERSTITIONE · EXPIATVM
NE · FORTITVDINIS · EORVM · EXCIDERET · MEMORIA
MONVMENT /M
A · CLEMENTE · X · PONT · MAX
AN · IVB MDCLXXV
PARIETINIS · DEALBATIS · DEPICTVM TEMPORVM · INIVRIA · DELETVM
BENEDICTVS · XIV · PONT · MAX
MARMOREVM · REDDI · CVRAVIT
AN · IVB · MDCCL · PONT · X
PIVS · IX · PONT · MAX
QVVM · PARTEM · MEDIAM · AD · ESQVILIAS · CONVERSAM
VETVSTATE · FATISCENTEM
RESTITVENDAM · ET · MVNIENDAM · CVRASSET
MEMORIAM · RENOVAVIT
ANNO MDCCCLII · PONT · VII

This plaque over an entrance to the Colosseum honors several popes for having the building repaired.

The nickname "Colosseum" came from a very large statue.

Romans starting calling the Flavian Amphitheater the Colosseum because of a huge statue right next door to the building. It was a statue of the former emperor Nero called the "Colossus of Nero." This statue was 120 feet (36.6 m) tall.

No one knows what happened to the Colossus of Nero. The statue's base, however, can still be seen in Rome.

FACT 5

More than 50,000 people could sit in the Colosseum. Once seats filled up, thousands more could stand.

When the Colosseum was built, between 50,000 and 55,000 people could sit to watch different events. If people were also standing on the floor, it may have held up to 87,000! Standing might have been more comfortable, since the seats were made of rock.

Full House!

stadium	city	how many people
Madison Square Garden	New York, NY	19,763
Staples Center	Los Angeles, CA	20,000
Fenway Park	Boston, MA	37,439
Yankee Stadium	Bronx, NY	50,287
Colosseum	Rome, Italy	55,000
Rose Bowl	Los Angeles, CA	92,542

Rose Bowl

FACT 6

The Colosseum wasn't just used for sports.

The most famous use of the Colosseum was the **gladiator** fights, which were a little like modern martial arts contests. There were many other types of shows there, though—from animal hunts to plays. It was also used for public **executions**.

Gladiators were men trained to fight other men or animals for public enjoyment. Many gladiators were slaves forced to fight, but others did it because they wanted to.

The Colosseum was sometimes turned into an ocean.

The Colosseum was sometimes used to re-create famous battles. To act out naval battles, the Romans flooded the Colosseum so the floor was entirely covered in deep water. Then, they staged famous sea battles using real ships!

Staged sea battles in ancient Rome were called *naumachia*. This comes from the Greek words for "naval battle."

13

This painting from the 1850s is titled *Ave Caesar Morituri te Salutant.* This means, "Hail Emperor Caesar, those who are about to die salute you."

FACT 8

Games at the Colosseum sometimes lasted for months.

Going to see a show at the Colosseum was a great way for ancient Romans to spend an afternoon. However, events at the Colosseum didn't always last just one afternoon. Special events and games could last up to 100 days!

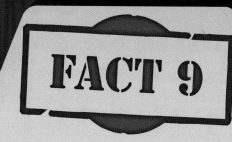

One celebration lasted 123 days.

In AD 107, 27 years after the Colosseum was finished, Emperor Trajan (TRAY-juhn) scored a major victory in battle. The **celebration** at the Colosseum was so big that it included 10,000 gladiators and 11,000 animals.

FACT 10

Some modern estimates say that almost half a million people died in the Colosseum.

The Colosseum was used for fake battles and gladiator fights over nearly 400 years. Some historians **estimate** that somewhere between 400,000 and 500,000 people died during events at the Colosseum.

FACT 11

Far more animals died in the Colosseum than people did.

Some historians estimate that more than a million wild animals were killed in games at the Colosseum. However, the gladiators didn't always win contests against animals. The animals were kept hungry for days to make sure the fight was exciting.

FACT 12

The Colosseum was the largest amphitheater built by the Roman Empire.

The Colosseum is 615 feet (187 m) long and 510 feet (155 m) wide. It covers about 6 acres (24,280 square m). The building is also more than 150 feet (46 m) tall. That's about 15 stories. The center arena was 287 by 180 feet (88 by 55 m).

Sizing Up the Colosseum

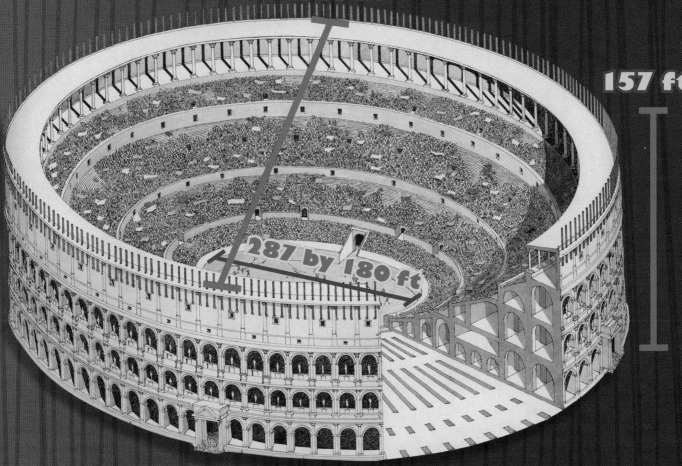

510 ft

157 ft

287 by 180 ft

615 ft

FACT 13

Everyone in a crowd entering the Colosseum could be seated in just 20 minutes.

Even though 50,000 people were trying to get into the building at once, it only took about 20 minutes to get everyone seated. This is because there were 84 different entrances and each one led directly to a section of seats.

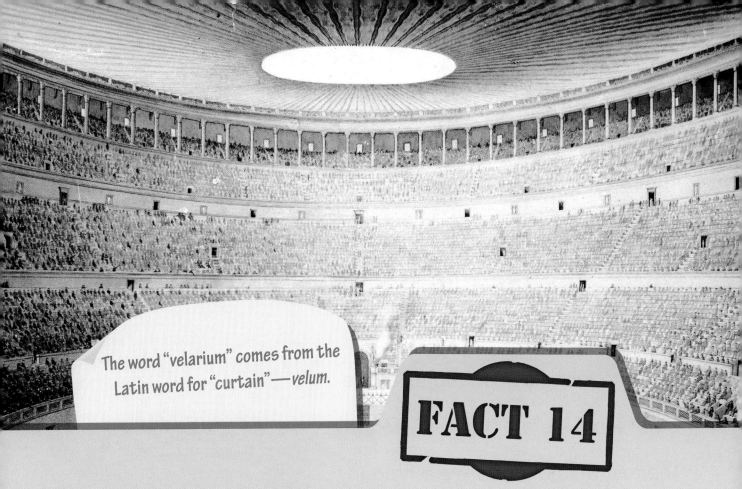

The word "velarium" comes from the Latin word for "curtain"—*velum*.

FACT 14

The Colosseum had a removable ceiling.

The makers of the Colosseum thought of everything. The building even had a large red **canvas** cover called the velarium. It was stretched over the top of the Colosseum to protect people from the sun and rain.

FACT 15

The Colosseum was used for games for less than a quarter of its life.

The last gladiator fights at the Colosseum were held in AD 435. The last animal hunts were held in AD 523. These events were ended because it cost too much to get new animals and train new gladiators.

For a while, the Colosseum was used as a living area for religious people.

FACT 16

After the fights ended, the Colosseum was used for many other things, including a fortress.

The Colosseum didn't just sit empty after the Romans stopped using it for entertainment. It was used for housing and workshops. Starting around 1200, it was used as a **fortress**. However, an earthquake in 1349 brought an end to that.

FACT 17

A large part of the original Colosseum is gone.

In 1349, a huge earthquake knocked down most of the southern end of the Colosseum. Fires over the years burned wooden beams supporting the building. More and more sections crumbled until major **restorations** took place in the 1800s.

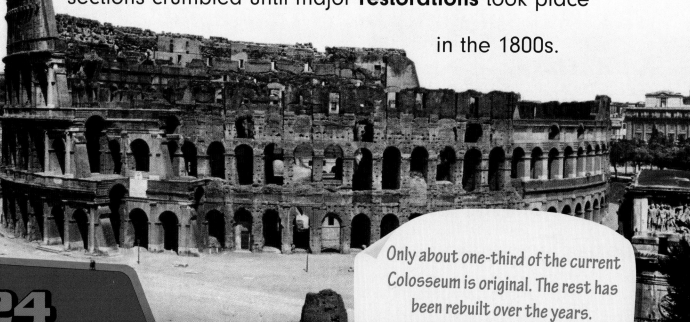

Only about one-third of the current Colosseum is original. The rest has been rebuilt over the years.

This painting—titled *The Colosseum, Rome by Daylight*—shows how it looked before restorations took place.

FACT 18

The Colosseum once looked like a jungle.

Before the restoration in 1871, more than 400 **species** of plants grew on the ruins. Where did all those plants come from? Many people think they came from fruit seeds in the waste of many kinds of animals brought to Rome from far away.

FACT 19

Parts of the Colosseum were used to build new buildings around Rome.

A strong, beautiful stone called marble was used to make many of the decorations in the Colosseum. Once the amphitheater fell into disuse, Romans used some of the marble to make other buildings, including St. Peter's Basilica—the Pope's church.

Work on St. Peter's began in 1506. It wasn't completed until 1615.

People dressed as Roman soldiers march past the Colosseum on April 21, 2013, during Rome's 2,766th anniversary celebration.

The Colosseum is still being used to entertain people.

Nearly 5 million people from around the world visit the Colosseum every year. The Colosseum has been in many movies since the 1950s, including *Roman Holiday*, *Way of the Dragon*, *Gladiator*, and *Madagascar 3: Europe's Most Wanted*.

Still Standing

Even though the Romans stopped using the Colosseum for games and festivals more than 1,400 years ago, it's still a popular and loved symbol of the Roman Empire. Recent efforts to restore this amazing building have opened up more areas to the public. It's even pictured on Italy's 5-cent euro coin.

The gladiator fights and wild animal hunts may have ended long ago, but the amazing story of the Colosseum continues to this day!

Even after 2,000 years, the Colosseum is still an impressive sight.

Glossary

amphitheater: a round or oval-shaped building with rising rows of seats and a central stage for events

canvas: a strong cloth used to make clothes, bags, tents, and other items

celebration: a time to show happiness for an event through activities such as eating or playing music

estimate: to make a careful guess about an answer based on the known facts

execution: the act of putting someone to death, especially as a legal punishment

fortress: a large, strong building made to protect a town or settlement

gladiator: a person who fought to the death for the entertainment of large crowds in ancient Rome

restoration: returning something to a former or original state

species: a group of plants or animals that are all of the same kind

stadium: a large building that has many rows of seats and is used for sporting events

statue: a work of art carved or shaped to look like a person or animal

For More Information

Books

Rose, Simon. *Colosseum*. New York, NY: Weigl Publishers, 2012.

Sonneborn, Liz. *The Romans: Life in Ancient Rome*. Minneapolis, MN: Millbrook Press, 2010.

Websites

The Colosseum: Emblem of Rome
www.bbc.co.uk/history/ancient/romans/colosseum_01.shtml
Read much more about the building and history of the Colosseum.

The Roman Colosseum
www.the-colosseum.net/idx-en.htm
This site is a fantastic resource for information on the Colosseum and the ancient Romans.

You Wouldn't Want to Be a Roman Gladiator!
www.salariya.com/web_books/gladiator/index.html
Find out what the life of a gladiator was really like at this fun interactive website.

Index

amphitheaters 4, 18, 26

animals 12, 15, 17, 22, 25, 28

battles 13, 15, 16

Colossus of Nero 9

earthquake 23, 24

entrances 20

executions 12

fights 5, 12, 16, 17, 22, 23, 28

fires 24

Flavian Amphitheater 8, 9

fortress 23

games 14, 17, 22, 28

gladiators 12, 15, 16, 17, 22, 28

housing 23

hunts 5, 12, 22, 28

movies 27

plants 25

plays 12

restorations 24, 25, 28

Roman Empire 4, 7, 18, 28

ruins 25

sea battles 13

shows 4, 7, 12, 14

size 18, 19

sports 4, 7, 12

stadiums 4, 6, 11

Titus 6, 8

Trajan 15

velarium 21

Vespasian 6, 8

visitors 27

workshops 23

JP
Cutler, Jane.
Darcy and Gran don't like babies.

"But you don't think that baby is like *you* were when *you* were a baby, do you, Gran?"

"Oh, yes, Darcy," Gran laughed, "I believe he is!"

"And deep down do *you* like the baby, Gran?"
"I believe I *might*," allowed Gran.

"And is it okay if you don't like the baby now?"

"I believe it will have to be,"
Gran said. She smiled.

"Do you think all the things
they say are right?" Darcy asked.
"I believe I do," said Gran.
"But what about you, Gran?"
"What about me, Darcy?"
"Are *you* going to like
the baby better later on?"

"I believe I will," said Gran.

"Our neighbor says I *do* like the baby," Darcy said.

Gran thought.
"I believe your neighbor means *deep down*," she said.

"The doctor says I'm not supposed
to like the baby," Darcy said.

Gran thought. "I believe the doctor means
it's okay if you don't," she said.

"Dad says I'll like the baby better
later on," Darcy said.
Gran thought.
"I believe that's true," she said.

"Mom says the baby is
just like I was," Darcy said.
Gran thought.
"I believe that's true," she said.

When the weather turned, they put on
their gloves and their hats and started home.

and climbed to the top of the jungle gym.

and slid down
the tall slide.

They rode on the teeter-totter

Darcy and Gran swung on the big swings

"Babies all over the place," grumbled Gran.
"It's okay, Gran," Darcy said.
"They can't do anything we want to do.
That's the one thing I like about babies."

When they got to the park,
they saw a lot of other people.
They saw a lot of babies.
The babies were in buggies.
The babies were in strollers.
The babies were in backpacks and frontpacks.
The babies were in mothers' arms.
The babies were on fathers' laps.
Some of the bigger babies
were in the sandbox, eating sand.
But not one baby was on the big swings.
Not one baby was on the tall slide.
Not one baby was on the teeter-totter.
Not one baby was on the jungle gym.
Not one baby was any place Darcy wanted to be.

Darcy and Gran put on their coats and their
walking shoes. Gran put their gloves and hats in
her backpack, in case the weather turned.
Off they marched to the playground.
Gran walked fast. So did Darcy.
Gran looked straight ahead. So did Darcy.
Gran breathed deeply. So did Darcy.

"Want to go to the park, Darcy?" Gran asked.
"There will be a lot of babies in the park," Darcy warned.
"They won't be on the big swings," Gran said.
"They won't be on the tall slide," Darcy agreed.
"They won't be on the teeter-totter," Gran pointed out.
"They won't be on the jungle gym," Darcy remembered.
"They won't be in our way," said Gran. "Let's go."

"What don't you like about them, Gran?" asked Darcy.
"I don't much like their smell
and I don't much like their looks," said Gran.
"I don't like all the work they make for everyone.
And besides, they get far too much attention."

Darcy had nothing more to say.

"I don't like the baby," Darcy told her Gran.

"Me neither," said Darcy's Gran.

"I never did like babies."

"I don't like the baby," Darcy told the neighbor.

"Of course you do," the neighbor said.

"I don't like the baby," Darcy told the doctor.

"You're not supposed to," said the doctor.

"I don't like the baby," Darcy told her father.

"You'll like him better later on, when he can do more things," Darcy's father said.

Darcy didn't care about later on.

"I don't like the baby," Darcy told her mother.

"But the baby is just like you were,
a long time ago," Darcy's mother said.

Darcy didn't care
about a long time ago.

When someone asked her
how she liked the baby,
she told them.

Pretty soon, no one asked.
But that didn't stop Darcy.

She didn't like his smell

and she didn't like his looks.

Darcy didn't like the baby.

For Linda Allen,
agent and
friend.
—J.C.

For my sister Nancy
and our nephews William
and David.
—S.R.

Library of Congress Cataloging-in-Publication Data

Cutler, Jane.
Darcy and Gran don't like babies / Jane Cutler;
illustrated by Susannah Ryan.
p.   cm.
Summary: Darcy and Gran are not happy about the idea of a new baby
coming, but they change their minds after the birth.
ISBN: 0-590-44587-1
[1. Babies—Fiction.   2. Brothers and sisters—Fiction.
3. Grandmothers—Fiction.]   I. Ryan, Susannah, ill.   II. Title.
PZ7.C985Dar   1991
[E]—dc20   91-42214
CIP
AC

12 11 10 9 8 7 6 5 4 3 2   3 4 5 6 7/9
Printed in the U.S.A.   36

First Scholastic printing, October 1993

Design by Claire B. Counihan

This artwork was drawn in charcoal and
painted with watercolor.

Darcy and Gran
Don't Like Babies

by JANE CUTLER

Illustrated by SUSANNAH RYAN

SCHOLASTIC
HARDCOVER

SCHOLASTIC INC. • New York

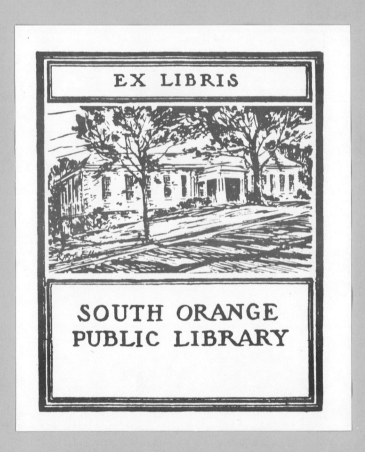

CONTENTS

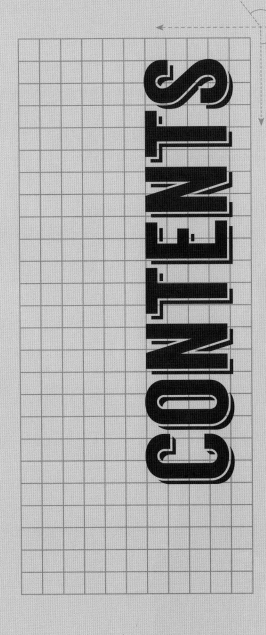

CHAPTER 1	A World without Print	6
	Timeline	15
CHAPTER 2	The Origins of Printing	16
CHAPTER 3	The Man from Mainz	28
CHAPTER 4	How Gutenberg Did It	38
CHAPTER 5	The Print Revolution	46
CHAPTER 6	Early American Printing	58
CHAPTER 7	The Age of Reason	70
CHAPTER 8	Technology Moves Forward	82
CHAPTER 9	The Digital Age	90

ESSENTIAL FACTS 100

GLOSSARY 102

ADDITIONAL RESOURCES 104

SOURCE NOTES 106

INDEX 110

ABOUT THE AUTHOR 112

CHAPTER 1

A WORLD WITHOUT PRINT

One evening in the 1440s, so the legend goes, Johann Gutenberg and his assistants nervously crowded around one of the printing presses in his shop in Mainz, Germany. Lines of inked metal type were fastened on the bed of the press. A sheet of damp paper was set into position directly above the type. Gutenberg told an assistant to turn the screw of the press. The top plate of the press came down slowly, touched the paper, and pressed it against the type. The assistant reversed the screw.

Turning the crank brings down the plate onto the paper in this replica of a Gutenberg press.

Gutenberg carefully lifted the paper from the type. He proudly looked at the crisp, clean lines of ink on the paper. He had unlocked the secrets of printing with movable type. The world would be forever changed.

Much of the knowledge the human race has gathered—history, science, philosophy, politics, religion, art and architecture, and more—is preserved and shared through the printed word. Books, magazines, newspapers, posters, maps, and other forms of printed material educate and entertain us daily. Although many of us take the printed word for granted, especially in the digital age, it is still almost impossible to imagine a world without print. Yet at one time, printing did not exist.

Before the Printed Word

Books existed long before the invention of the printing press in the mid-1400s. Many of the world's greatest works of literature were written long before printing appeared. The ancient Egyptians, Greeks, and Romans produced classic works that are still read to this day. Medieval English writers produced many dramas and stories that are considered masterpieces of world literature. Throughout Europe, Latin translations of the Bible and other religious texts were available. Various forms of literature, accounts of daily life, and histories appeared in many parts of Asia and the New World.

Before printing, books were copied by hand, one by one. Scribes labored in royal courts, universities, and monasteries and abbeys. They painstakingly copied texts while artists created illustrations to adorn their work. In France, as many as 10,000 scribes worked to meet the needs of churches, courts, and universities at the beginning of the 1400s.[1] England's chancery, responsible for producing official government documents, employed 60 copyists.[2]

A scribe's labor was tedious, and it frequently took months to produce a single copy of a text. Even the most highly skilled scribes made errors, omitting or adding words to the text. Some scribes used their own system of abbreviations, which often made readings of the text inaccurate. Translating text from Latin into another language, such as German or English, also increased the likelihood of errors.

PREHISTORIC COMMUNICATION

From the time the earliest humans roamed Earth, people have had a strong desire to communicate with their fellow beings. Thousands of years before writing appeared, humans created primitive drawings and paintings. Some of the earliest examples of prehistoric art are the cave paintings in Lascaux, France. The more than 15,000 figures depict animals, humans, and abstract signs that researchers date back 17,000 years.[3] Petroglyphs, or rock carvings, have been found in all parts of the world. Archaeologists have estimated some petroglyphs found in Western Australia are up to 30,000 years old.[4]

Cy co̅mece le iij.e liure du regime et gouuernemēnt des princes

O ignorance inbeallite e rudesse de mō tāt multrae en
tendent q̃ pourm maintenat ma tāt mexteruce mas
those digne destre seue visitec ne regardee par la treshaul
te sacuate prudente e hault sauoir de celuy qui est mi
rouer de noblesse source de vertus pure de scauoir fontai
ne delaquence. O tresmepte n̄false et indigerec escripte
de moy hors de toute facōde claquece et ornee rethoriq̃
Cōmt seras tu st audacteuse ne haedre de toy prūter de
nāt si treshaute e trespuissāte serenite e selatiide. Prez
ton aduocate et intercesceresse sa benignite doulceur et clemēce pourpatro
ciner entuers luy toy donner graueux assez et affable vertuel pour luy pre
senter tō opuscule e petit traicte fait e compille en lhonne̅ et reuerence

THE MANUSCRIPT

A handwritten document is also called a manuscript. The word *manuscript* comes from the Latin words *manu*, "hand," and *scriptus*, "to write." Manuscripts were written on specially prepared animal skins or plant fibers. The oldest known manuscripts date to ancient Egypt, although manuscripts were produced in ancient times in Asia, the Middle East, Europe, and South America. The Dead Sea Scrolls, discovered in 1947 in a cave near Qumran, Israel, is a collection of manuscripts roughly 2,200 years old. The texts, written in Hebrew and Aramaic, offer a glimpse into religious and cultural aspects of Jewish life during that time. Most of the manuscripts that survive from the Middle Ages are religious books that reflect the beliefs and practices of Christianity, Judaism, and Islam. The British Library in London and the National Library of France house two of the world's largest collections of medieval manuscripts.

The process of hand copying was expensive, a service only the wealthy and the church could afford. Furthermore, scribes eventually were unable to meet the demands of the government, universities, and the clergy for written material.

Yet for years—often in secret—some clever individuals in Europe were hard at work trying to develop a faster and more efficient way of reproducing texts and images. Among them was a little-known metalworker from the German town of Mainz.

Medieval manuscripts were works of art, but they were costly and slow to produce.

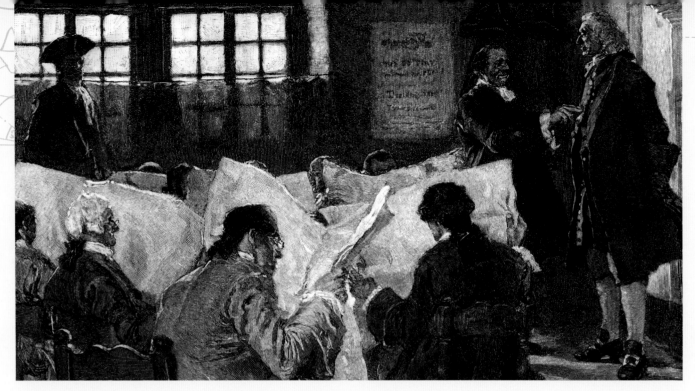

The quick dissemination of news helped propel Europe into the modern era.

Who Was Gutenberg?

Very few details are known about the early life of Johann Gutenberg. It is certain he was born in Mainz, but the exact date of his birth is unknown. Much of what we know about his later life comes from the records of court cases in which he was involved.

By the late 1430s, accounts of Gutenberg's life indicate that he had begun work on some form of mechanical means that could reproduce texts in large quantities. Witness testimony from a lawsuit brought against him in 1439 shows he was already engaged in developing some kind of a printing process. Eventually—with years of hard work marked by lawsuits and business failures—Gutenberg devised a printing machine and a printing process.

A Force of Change

Printing spread across Europe like wildfire. By the end of the 1400s—less than 50 years after Gutenberg's creation first appeared—236 towns had printing presses. More than 35,000 editions of books had been published, amounting to 15 to 20 million copies.[5]

The printing press became the primary technology for communication, and the printed word became a powerful force for change. Knowledge spread quickly across Europe through all forms of print—books, pamphlets, maps, charts, and diagrams. The availability of printed material improved the education process, as more and more people learned to read. Printed contracts and business documents made commerce and trade easier.

The printing press also made it easier to spread knowledge accurately. Errors introduced into texts by scribes became a thing of the past. Now it was

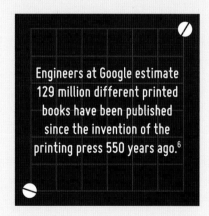

Engineers at Google estimate 129 million different printed books have been published since the invention of the printing press 550 years ago.[6]

13

Printing helped a culture of literacy spread.

possible for identical copies of a book to be sold in France, England, or any other country. Printers kept lists of errata, or errors, discovered in books after they were printed. The next time the book was printed, the errors were fixed and the corrected information appeared in the book.

The technology of the printing press increased literacy by cutting the cost of book production and making the printed word available to a wider audience. New ideas affected how people thought about themselves, their societies, and the world. New attitudes led to changes in society. Printing changed the world.

THE PRINTING PRESS

ca. 3200 BCE
Writing begins in Egypt and Mesopotamia.

105 CE
Court official Ts'ai Lun invents paper in China.

c. 1041
Chinese inventor Pi Sheng makes movable type from hardened clay.

1440s
Johann Gutenberg uses movable type in Mainz, Germany.

c. 1475
William Caxton prints the first book in England, which begins standardizing the English language.

1543
First works by Copernicus and Vesalius are published.

c. 1638
The first printing press is established in North America, in Massachusetts.

1796
German playwright Alois Senefelder invents lithography.

1812
Friedrich Koenig invents a steam-powered cylinder press.

1844
Richard Hoe invents a rotary printing press.

1884
Ottmar Mergenthaler invents the Linotype machine.

1904
Ira Rubel develops the process of offset printing.

c. 1940s
The Xerox Corporation develops the copier.

1960s
Computers provide electronic typesetting and electronic book production.

1980s—present
Desktop publishing ushers in a new era of digital printing.

CHAPTER 2

THE ORIGINS OF
PRINTING

W riting developed in Mesopotamia (present-day Iraq) and Egypt in approximately 3200 BCE, thousands of years before printing appeared. As these societies developed and became more complex, the need for improved communication increased.

The Origins of Writing

The Sumerians of Mesopotamia recorded business dealings, including the trading of animals, weapons, and tools. Using the end of a sharply cut reed, scribes drew simple pictures of an item on wet clay tablets. A scratch or slit indicated the number counted and

One form of writing developed in ancient Egypt thousands of years ago.

recorded. When set out to bake in the sun or in ovens, the tablet hardened and became a permanent document. Later the symbols came to represent syllable sounds. This writing developed in Mesopotamia is called cuneiform. The term comes from the Latin word *cuneus*, "wedge," referring to the wedge-shaped marks made by the reed in the damp clay.

The Egyptians developed a writing system shortly after the Sumerians. The characters used in early ancient Egyptian writing, however, were more picture-like than cuneiform. Egyptian writing is known as hieroglyphics. Egyptian temples, tombs, and public buildings were beautifully decorated with this writing and other art. Eventually, the Egyptians developed writing that was quicker and easier to use, and hieroglyphics were used only on monuments.

An important milestone in the development of ancient Egyptian writing was the development of papyrus as a writing surface. Made from a plant that grows along the Nile River, papyrus provided a flexible, smooth surface on which scribes could write neatly. When pasted together, sheets of papyrus formed long rolls called scrolls. Using hundreds of different images, scribes recorded all aspects of Egyptian culture: religion, politics, business, warfare, and daily life.

Writing appeared in the Indus River valley (present-day Pakistan and western India) in approximately 2500 BCE. The characters of Indus writing include pictures and

There are roughly 500,000 Mesopotamian cuneiform tablets held in museums around the world. The British Museum in London, England, has the largest collection, with approximately 130,000 tablets.[1]

abstract signs. Most examples of Indus writing appear on flat carved stones called seals, but they also have been found on tools, pottery, and copper plates. No one today knows how to decipher this writing.

Chinese writing is believed to date back to 1600 BCE. In the ancient Chinese system, thousands of ideograms, or individual signs and symbols, were used. Each symbol represented a different word or concept. Although Chinese writing has evolved substantially over the centuries, it still features a complex system of thousands of characters.

The Coming of the Alphabet

A critical turning point in the history of writing was the development of the phonetic alphabet. By approximately 1500 BCE, a group from the Eastern Mediterranean, possibly the Phoenicians, devised an alphabet of consonants. The alphabet had an enormous impact on world culture. No longer would a person have to learn the meaning of hundreds or thousands of characters to understand the written word. By 950 BCE, the Greeks had adopted the Phoenician alphabet and added vowels. Within 300 years, the Greeks developed the basis of the alphabets used in the Western world today.

The alphabet was a boon to writing and the spread of knowledge. Writing on papyrus and parchment, Greek scribes produced approximately 400,000 manuscripts in 300 years.[2] Among the treasured parchments were Plato's

A WONDER OF THE ANCIENT WORLD

The Great Library in Alexandria, Egypt, was one of the largest and most important libraries of the ancient world. Most scholars believe Ptolemy Soter, a Greek general and ruler of Egypt from 323 to 283 BCE, created the library. The library's collection consisted of approximately 400,000 to 700,000 papyrus rolls dedicated to areas of study such as medicine, mathematics, astronomy, engineering, and biology.[3] Official written versions of classic Greek plays and dramas were also housed in the library. Modern experts agree numerous fires and destructive acts over the centuries eventually destroyed the library. By the end of the 300s CE, the library was no longer in operation.

Republic and works by Euclid, Aristotle, and Herodotus. Many of these classic works were stored in the library at Alexandria, Egypt, and made available to scholars all over the world.

By the 600s BCE, the Romans had adopted a form of the Greek alphabet and made it suitable for writing the Latin language. As the Roman Empire expanded across Europe, the Roman alphabet spread with it.

As did the Egyptians, the ancient Greeks and Romans wrote mainly on papyrus and, in later years, parchment. As the volume of writing increased throughout Europe, there was an increased demand for both types of writing surfaces.

Papyrus was inexpensive to make, but it wore out quickly and deteriorated in humid climates. Papyrus manuscripts have survived to this day only in Egypt and other dry locations. Parchment was more durable, but it was also expensive and time-consuming to produce.

Greek was the language of scholarship for hundreds of years.

Skins of sheep, cows, or goats were washed in water. The hairs of the hide were removed by soaking the skins in a special solution. A worker scraped away the hair with a blade. The skins were rubbed smooth with a stone, allowed to dry, rubbed with chalk, and finished with a lime-based wash. It took many animal skins to make one book. Parchment was also thicker than papyrus, causing parchment manuscripts to be far heavier than ones made of papyrus. A better writing material was needed.

PERMANENT INK

Chinese inventors continued making improvements in the writing and printing process. In the mid-200s, Wei Tan developed a durable ink by mixing oil with black soot collected from burning candlewicks. The ink was ideal for writing with a brush—the preferred writing tool of scribes and monks—and its dark color made the ink nearly permanent. Today we know this ink as Chinese or India ink, and artists still use it for drawing.

Asia Leads the Way

Meanwhile, in China, political official Ts'ai Lun was developing a remarkable material that would eventually make both papyrus and parchment obsolete. In 105 CE, Ts'ai Lun boiled tree bark, hemp, rags, and fishnets together in a pot. He pounded the soaking materials into a thick paste, which he spread in a thin layer across a wooden screen. Left out to dry in the sun, the moisture in the substance drained through the screen, and the material dried into a thin, rigid sheet. Ts'ai Lun's paper was cheaper to make, easier to store, and more versatile than papyrus and parchment. But it would be hundreds of years before paper spread beyond Asia.

By the 700s, the Chinese had developed block printing, which allowed them to reproduce images on paper. Artists drew an image onto a block of wood and carved away the areas that were to show white at the printing stage. The printer then applied ink to the raised surface of the block and pressed sheets of paper on top of it. In later years, words

The Derge Parkhang print shop in Tibet still prints using hand-carved wood blocks as it did when it was founded in 1729.

were added to block prints, and eventually complete pages of texts were carved onto wooden blocks. Block printing soon spread throughout the region.

Movable Type

Block printing was a slow and tedious process. Once a block was carved, it could be used to print only one page, although in multiple copies. A printer had to carve a new block for each page.

THE COMING OF THE CODEX

The development of paper led to a new technology: the codex. Beginning in the 100s CE, handwritten sheets were no longer pasted or sewn together to form a long continuous scroll. Instead, several sheets were placed on top of each other, folded down the middle, and stitched or bound together with thread or leather thongs so that they opened into pages. Several gatherings of sheets could be sewn together to create a larger book. Leather covers were bound around the pages to protect them. This basic technology is still used in bookmaking today—nearly 2,000 years after it first appeared.

In approximately 1041, Chinese blacksmith and printer Pi Sheng devised a solution to the problem: movable type. Pi Sheng made his type by carving characters into moist clay and baking the blocks until the clay hardened. But instead of using a single large printing block with many characters carved into it, Pi Sheng made many smaller blocks with one character on each. The smaller blocks, called type, could be pieced together to print a page. Then they could be taken apart and rearranged to create an entirely new page.

At the end of the 1300s, Chinese and Korean printers began using type made of metal. The Koreans created type by pouring liquid metal into molds of different shapes and characters. When the metal cooled, it was in the shape of the mold, ready to be inked and used for printing. This process of making type from melted and reshaped metal is called casting. One historian of the time noted, "There will be no book left unprinted, and no man who does not learn. Literature and religion will make daily progress, and the cause of morality must gain enormously."[4]

However, the enormous number of characters and images in the Chinese and Korean systems of writing made even this new form of printing impractical. To solve the problem, King Sejong the Great of Korea oversaw the creation of a new alphabet with approximately two dozen letters. But scholars were reluctant to use the new alphabet, and common people had no way of learning it. Many Korean printers preferred block printing. Printing with movable type ended in Korea around 1544 and did not appear again until 1770.

European Developments

By the early 1300s, block printing on paper had appeared in Europe. Some of the earliest known European block prints feature religious themes. Another common product of block printing was the playing card. Gutenberg may have known about block printing and block-printed images, known as woodcuts. By the mid-1400s, entire books were being block printed in many parts of Europe.

THE OLDEST BOOK

The Chinese used the block printing technique to create the world's oldest surviving printed book. In 868, Wang Jie printed *The Diamond Sutra*, a collection of religious teachings. The book is in a roll 16 feet (5 m) long and one foot (0.3 m) wide, made up of six sheets of paper, each approximately 30 inches (76 cm) long, glued end to end. A seventh shorter sheet has an illustration.

Medieval books were expensive and slow to produce, but many still survive today.

During this time, scribes continued producing manuscripts. Much of the work produced in the late Middle Ages was Christian scriptures and religious texts, especially the Bible. While most manuscripts were written on parchment, some monasteries and commercial workshops began using paper as a writing surface. Arab traders who had contact with China and the Far East introduced the craft of papermaking to Italy in the 1100s. By the time Gutenberg began to work on his printing press, paper mills were operating in most major cities in Europe.

In the late Middle Ages, serious students learned to read and write Latin, the language in which most books were written. As universities sprouted up across Europe, there was an increased need for books and other printed materials. These higher centers of learning produced well-educated, well-trained lawyers, doctors, teachers, and scholars.

By the early 1500s, many publishers had staffs of translators converting Latin into various local vernaculars. Some of the more popular books included works by ancient Romans and handsomely crafted deluxe editions of the Bible created for the wealthy. Yet book production remained slow and costly. A bookseller could make a fortune if he could produce books quickly and inexpensively!

THE BEAUTY OF THE BOOK

Manuscripts were often decorated with magnificent color illustrations and ornate hand lettering. These books were known as illuminated manuscripts. The scribes and monks copying texts frequently made the first letter of a section of text larger than the rest and decorated it with colored ink. Many times they also drew tiny pictures within and around the initial letters. Copyists also decorated pages with bright, colorful borders featuring geometric patterns, animal wildlife, and plants and vines. The *Lindisfarne Gospels*, produced around 700 CE on the British island of Lindisfarne, and the *Book of Kells*, created in Ireland approximately 100 years later, are two of the most beautiful illuminated manuscripts ever made.

CHAPTER 3

THE MAN FROM MAINZ

Johann Gutenberg was born into a wealthy landowning family in Mainz, Germany, in approximately 1400. His father, Friele, was an eminent citizen of the city, serving as a town councillor. He also worked at the mint where coins were manufactured. Johann may have learned about metals at the mint.

Johann's mother, Else Wirich or Wyrich, was Friele's second wife. Else was the daughter of a shopkeeper, although she had inherited a country estate six miles (10 km) from Mainz. Johann had an older brother, Friele, and an older sister, Else, both named for their parents.

A statue that memorializes Gutenberg stands in Mainz.

MEDIEVAL CRAFT GUILDS

During the Middle Ages, craftsmen and merchants often formed groups known as craft guilds. Similar to modern-day unions, members of each craft joined together to regulate the wages, working conditions, and production techniques of their craft. In the 1400s, the city of Mainz had many guilds. Each guild was organized into three levels. Masters were the highest-skilled craftsmen in the guild. A master owned workshops and trained apprentices in return for a sizable fee. Apprentices received no wages. After working for several years, an apprentice moved up to the level of journeyman, where he could work for other masters and receive payment for his labor. In many European towns, guilds were politically active, and in some cases, they gained control of the local government.

Magic Mirrors and Secret Arts

There was trouble in the city during Gutenberg's childhood. Tensions between patricians and guild members flared over money. In response, in 1411, more than 100 patricians—including the Gutenbergs—fled Mainz to live on their estates outside the city. Johann and his family likely retreated to Else's family home at Eltville. The archbishop of Mainz negotiated a compromise, however, and the patricians returned to the city. But Mainz remained sharply divided, and the Gutenbergs left for safety again in 1413.

In his late teen years, Gutenberg returned to Mainz, where he remained for a time after his father's death in 1419. When conflicts with the guilds erupted again, he moved to Strasbourg sometime between 1429 and 1434. Strasbourg was a center of metal crafts. Gutenberg settled in a small village outside Strasbourg's city walls. In 1438, he decided he would manufacture small metal badges with mirrors to sell to pilgrims venturing to a popular shrine in Aachen, Germany. The pilgrims believed the mirrors captured the healing powers of the holy relics displayed at the shrine.

Gutenberg acquired three partners to carry out his plan. In approximately 1438, he signed a contract with Hans Riffe, Andreas Dritzehn, and Andreas Heilmann to form a business. Each of the three men invested money in the mirror venture for a share of the profits. Evidence possibly suggests the mirrors were cast from a mixture of metals Gutenberg would later use in casting type. Work progressed until roughly the summer of 1438, when an outbreak of the black plague in the region halted the pilgrims until 1440.

The partners suspected that Gutenberg was hiding secrets related to his printing activities, so the four men entered into a new contract in which Gutenberg "should conceal from them none of the arts he knew."[1] The five-year agreement stated that if one of the partners died, his heirs would receive only a small portion of the deceased's original investment. All four partners were sworn to secrecy about the project.

Gutenberg hired Konrad Saspach or Sasbach, a local carpenter, to build a press to Gutenberg's specifications and set it up at Dritzehn's house. Saspach likely modified the design of some type of screw press, similar to those used in wine or olive oil production.

A museum curator shows how a replica Gutenberg press works.

In late December 1438, Andreas Dritzehn died at a friend's house. Gutenberg told Saspach to go to Dritzehn's house and take apart certain pieces of the press. But when Saspach arrived, the equipment was gone. Dritzehn's brothers Claus and George demanded that Gutenberg pay them Andreas's share in the partnership. When Gutenberg refused, the brothers insisted on entering into the partnership. Gutenberg refused again, and George sued him. In December 1439, the court ruled Gutenberg should repay the brothers a small sum, but the rest of the money would stay in the venture. Gutenberg was free to continue his work, but more important, his secret remained under wraps.

Last Days at Strasbourg and Back to Mainz

Little is known about what Gutenberg and his remaining partners, Hans Riffe and Andreas Heilmann, did for the next three years. Perhaps they manufactured and sold the pilgrim mirrors, although no samples of Gutenberg's mirrors have ever been found. In 1443, the partners' five-year contract expired, and the partnership broke up.

In 1444, Gutenberg left Strasbourg and disappeared from the public record for the next four years. Exactly what he did during that time remains a mystery.

Gutenberg was back in Mainz by 1448, at which time he borrowed money from his cousin Arnold Gelthus. Some historians believe the borrowed funds may have allowed Gutenberg to finance another small workshop with several former assistants from Strasbourg. He likely brought to Mainz any printer's tools he had made in Strasbourg.

Gutenberg was at last ready for his first publishing venture. His earliest work was the *Donatus*, one of the most widely used books of the 1400s. The Latin grammar book was possibly the one he had used himself in school. His second project was the publication of the German poem *The Sibylline Prophecies*, about the life of Jesus Christ and the history of the Church. Gutenberg hoped sales of the two books would provide him with the money to finance his dream project: printing the Bible.

A later artist imagined Gutenberg, *left*, Fust, *center*, and an assistant at work at the press.

A New Partner

In approximately 1449, Gutenberg met Johann Fust, a wealthy goldsmith and merchant. After learning of Fust's interest in Latin and German books, Gutenberg may have shown his new friend pages of the *Donatus* that he was printing. Convinced Gutenberg's new invention could be highly profitable, Fust lent the printer money to buy new equipment.

Gutenberg built new presses, purchased metals, and trained workers. Meanwhile, he continued perfecting his techniques of creating typefaces and casting metal type. In 1452, Fust made a second loan, but it came with an important condition: if Gutenberg could not repay both loans at the completion of the project, Fust would seize all the equipment and supplies Gutenberg bought with the loan money. Gutenberg hired Peter Schoeffer, an experienced scribe and manuscript illuminator, as foreman of his print shop.

Gutenberg and his assistants worked for nearly five years to print 180 copies of the Bible; 30 were printed on vellum and the rest on paper. Each copy contained more than 1,280 pages in two volumes.[2] Each vellum copy required 170 calfskins.[3] The text on each page of the Bible was neatly arranged in two columns of 42 lines each. It was a masterpiece and proved beyond the shadow of a doubt the efficiency of Gutenberg's invention. By the end of the century, a printer could produce in a month what it would have taken a scribe a lifetime to copy.

THE GUTENBERG BIBLE BY THE NUMBERS

1,286:	Number of pages in each completed Bible
300:	Unique letters or characters seen in the Bible
2,500:	Average letters or characters on each page, each needing its own piece of metal type
3-5:	Number of years it took to complete printing
14 lbs (6.3 kg):	Weight of each Bible
30 Florins:	Selling price of the Bible; roughly three years of an average clerk's wage
49:	Number of copies of the Bible known to exist today. Of the 49 copies of the Gutenberg Bible known to exist, only 21 are complete.[4]

PETER SCHOEFFER, MASTER TECHNICIAN

Peter Schoeffer was an expert technician and skilled copyist who served as Gutenberg's primary assistant in Mainz. In approximately 1449, he went to Paris, where he worked as a calligrapher and copyist at the city's university. By 1452, Schoeffer returned to Germany and Gutenberg hired him.

When Fust gained control of Gutenberg's shop, he chose Schoeffer to run the operation. Together the two men created a thriving printing and publishing business, and Schoeffer married Fust's daughter, Christina. He successfully continued the business under his own name after Fust died in 1466.

In 1455, as work on the Bible neared completion, Fust sued Gutenberg for failing to repay the loans. After a hearing, the court ordered Gutenberg to repay only part of the loan, but even that was far more than Gutenberg could scrape together. Fust seized Gutenberg's presses, his type, and every copy of the nearly completed Bible. Fust installed Schoeffer as head of a new printing operation. Several months later, Fust and Schoeffer issued their Bible.

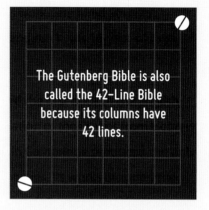

The Gutenberg Bible is also called the 42-Line Bible because its columns have 42 lines.

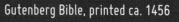

Gutenberg Bible, printed ca. 1456

non fuisse ausum affirmare se raptū
in lege in dixisse : siue in corpore siue extra corp² nescio deus scit. Hijg in-
teralibus argumentis apocryphas in libro ecclesie fabulas arguebat. Suprā
qua qª lectoris arbitrio iudicii dereliquit
quētē illud āmoneo nō habri danielem apud hebreos inter ppheias:
sed inter eos qui agiographa cōscri-
psisere. In tres siquidē partes omniu
ab ijs scriptura diuiditur : in legē
in prophetas et in agiographa id est
in quinq; et in octo et in undecim libros
quo nō est huj² tēporis disserere. Qua
aut p hoc, ppheta : nō contra hūc
librū porphyrius obicit testre sunt
methodus eusebius apollinaris : qui
multis uersuū milibus eius uesanie respondens nescio an curioso lectori satis-
fecerint. Unde obsecro uos o paula et
eustochiū fundatis , ꝓ me ad dūm pre-
ces : ut quādiu in hoc corpusculo ꝓ sū
da aliquid gratū uobis uile ecclesie ti-
biq; pstiro. Presentem quippe iudicij
oblataū nō sane mouear : si in utra
que parte aut amore labuntur aut odio.

Explicit prologus.

Anno tertio regni io-
achim regis iuda ve-
nit nabuchodonosor
rex babilonis iheru-
salem et obsedit eam.
Et tradidit dominus
in manu ei² ioachim regē iude et parte
uasorū domus dei : et asportauit ea in
terrā sennaar in domū dei sui : uasa
intulit in domū thesauri dei sui. Et ait
rex asfanez ꝓposito eunuchorū ut intro-
ducret de filijs isrl et de semine regio
et tyrannorū pueros : in quibus nulla esset
macula decoros forma et eruditos omni sapiētia cautos scientia et doctos

disciplina : et qui possent stare in pala-
tio regis : ut doceret eos litteras et lin-
guam chaldeorū. Et cōstituit eis rex an-
nonā per singulos dies de cibis suis
et de uino unde bibebat ipse : ut enutri-
ti tribus annis postea starent in cōspectu
regis. Fuerunt ergo inter eos de filijs iude daniel ananias misahel et azarias.
Et imposuit eis ꝓpositus eunuchorū
nomina danieli balthasar : ananie
sidrac misaheli misac et azarie abde-
nago. Proposuit aut daniel in corde
suo ne polluretur de mensa regis neq;
de uino potus ei² : et rogauit eunuchorū
ꝓpositum ne contaminaretur. Dedit aut deus danieli gratiam et misericordiam
in cōspectu principis eunuchorū. Et ait
princeps eunuchorū ad danielē. Timeo
ego dūm meū regē qui cōstituit uobis
cibū et potū : qui si uiderit uultus uros
macilentiores pre ceteris adolescentibus
coeuis uestris : condemnabitis caput
meū regi. Et dixit daniel ad malassar
quē cōstituerat princeps eunuchorū super danielem ananiā misahelē et aza-
riam. Tempta nos obsecro seruos tuos
diebus decē et dentur nobis legumina
ad uescendū et aqua ad bibendū : et
cōtemplare uultus nostros et uultus
puerorū qui uescuntur cibo regio : et si-
cut uideris facias cū seruis tuis. Qui
audito sermone huiuscemodi tempta-
uit eos diebus decem. Post dies aut decem apparuerunt uultus eorū meliores
et corpulentiores : pre omnibus pueris
qui uescebantur cibo regio. Porro malassar tollebat cibaria et uinū potus
eorū : dabatq; eis legumina. Pueris
aut his dedit deus scientiā et disciplinā
in omni libro et sapientia : danieli
aut intelligentiā omnium uisionum et
somniorū. Completis itaq; diebus

post quos dixerat rex ut introducerē-
tur : introduxit eos ꝓpositus eunuchorū
in cōspectu nabuchodonosor. Cumq;
eos locut² fuisset rex : nō sunt inuenti ta-
les de uniuersis ut daniel ananias misahel et azarias. Et steterunt in cōspectu regis : et omne uerbum sapientie
et intellectus quod sciscitatus est ab eis
inuenit in eis decuplum super cunctos
ariolos et magos qui erant in uni-
uerso regno eius. Fuit autem daniel
usq; ad annū primū cyri regis.

In anno secundo regni nabuchodonosor
uidit nabuchodonosor somniū : et cō-
territus est spirit² ei² et somniū ei²
fugit ab eo. Precepit aut rex ut cōuo-
carentur arioli et magi et malefici et
chaldei : ut indicarent regi somnia sua.
Qui cū uenissent steterunt corā rege.
Et dixit ad eos rex. Uidi somniū : et
mente confusus ignoro quid uiderim. Re-
sponderunt chaldei regi syriace. Rex
in sempiternū uiue. Dic somniū tuū
seruis tuis : et interpretationem eius
indicabimus. Et respondens rex ait chaldeis.
Sermo recessit a me. Nisi indicaueritis mihi
somniū et cōiecturā ei² : peribitis uos :
et domus uestre publicabuntur. Si aut
somniū et cōiecturā ei² narraueritis :
premia et dona et honorē multū acci-
pietis a me. Somniū igitur et interpretationem eius indicate mihi. Respōde-
runt secundo atq; dixerunt. Rex somniū
dicat seruis suis : et interpretationem eius
indicabimus. Respōdit rex et ait. Certe
noui q² tempus redimitis : scientes q² re-
cesserit a me sermo. Si ergo somniū
nō indicaueritis mihi una est de uobis
sententia : q² interpretationem quoq; fal-
lacem et deceptione plenā cōposueri-
tis ut loquamini mihi donec tempus
pertranseat. Somniū itaq; dicite mihi :

ut sciam q² interpretationem quoq; eius
ueram loquamini. Respondentes ergo
chaldei corā rege dixerunt. Nō est homo
super terrā qui sermonem tuū rex possit
implere : sed neq; regum quisquā ma-
gnus et potens uerbū huiuscemodi sci-
scitatur ab omni ariolo et mago et chal-
deo. Sermo enim quē tu querie rex gra-
uis est : nec reperietur quisquā qui indi-
cet illud in cōspectu regis excepto dijs
quorū nō est cōuersatio cū hominibus.
Quo audito : rex in furore et in ira ma-
gna precepit ut perirent omnes sapientes babilonis. Et egressa sententia sapientes interficiebantur : querebaturq;
daniel et socij eius ut perirent. Tunc daniel requisiuit de lege atq; sententia ab
arioch principe militie regis qui egres-
sus fuerat ad interficiendos sapientes
babilonis. Et interrogauit eum qui a rege potestatem acceperat : quā ob cau-
sam tam crudelis sentētia a facie regis
esset egressa. Cū ergo rem indicasset a-
rioch danieli : daniel ingressus rogauit
regem ut tempus daret sibi ad solutionē
indicandā regi. Et ingressus est domū
suam : ananias et misahel et azarias
socijs suis indicauit negotiū ut quererent
misericordiā a facie dei celi super sacra-
mento isto : et nō perirent daniel et socij
eius cū ceteris sapientibus babilonis.
Tunc danieli misteriū p uisione noctis
reuelatū est. Et daniel benedixit deo celi
et locutus ait. Sit nomen dūi benedi-
ctum a seculo et usq; in seculū : quia sapientia et fortitudo eius sunt. Et ipse
mutat tempora et etates : transfert reg-
na atq; constituit : dat sapientiam
sapientibus : et scientiā intelligentibus di-
sciplinam. Ipse reuelat ꝓfunda et absco-
dita : et nouit in tenebris constituta : et
lux cum eo est. Tibi deus patrū nostrorū

CHAPTER 4

HOW GUTENBERG DID IT

S cholars suggest Gutenberg had to solve three problems in order to reproduce books with a machine. He needed an ink that could be put on metal surfaces and transferred to paper under pressure. He required a press for bringing the inked metal into contact with paper. And most challenging, he had to create the materials and a process for making movable metal type. Without any of these essentials in place, Gutenberg's efforts would be doomed to failure.

A set of movable types requires multiple copies of each letter so there are enough of each to lay out a full page at a time.

NEW INK

Gutenberg discovered the typical water-based ink of his time ran off the metal typefaces when it was applied. He needed a thicker substance that would spread evenly with minimum effort. After repeated attempts, he finally developed an oil-based paint that included black soot, copper, lead, titanium, sulfur, and oil. Gutenberg's ink has a glittering, glossy quality that is similar to varnish.

Making the Type

Gutenberg needed tens of thousands of pieces of type to print with: he had to make a separate piece of type for *each* letter in *each* word on any page. To do this, Gutenberg had a craftsman carve a metal punch for each character—letters, numbers, and punctuation marks. The punch was two to three inches (5 to 7.6 cm) long, with the character engraved and filed on the end. Each character had to be perfect because tens of thousands of pieces of type would be made from the one punch. Each type would be an exact copy of the original punch.

A workman hammered the punch deeply into a piece of softer metal, called a strike, leaving an indentation. This strike was then filed to smooth and flatten its surface to remove any pieces of metal raised by the driven punch. This was called justifying the matrix and was a highly skilled task. The justified piece of metal was called the matrix, a word taken from the Latin *mater*, or "mother." The matrix would be the receptacle into which liquid metal would be poured to form the character.

The next step was making the casting chamber, or mold, for the matrix. The mold had to produce the raised image of a letter in reverse as well as a stem (the body) to hold the letter. Every piece of type for each different character had to be exactly the same height. If not, only the taller letters would make contact with the paper during printing. To ensure that each line of type was straight and parallel to the others, the baseline of the letter had to be the same as all the other pieces of type. To compound the problem, the width of each piece of type had to vary because letters such as *l* and *i* are narrower than letters such as *m* and *w*.

To solve the dilemma, Gutenberg devised an adjustable handheld mold that provided a uniform height for letters, but varying widths. He made two L-shaped pieces that slid together so the spaces between them could be adjusted. Therefore, the mold could

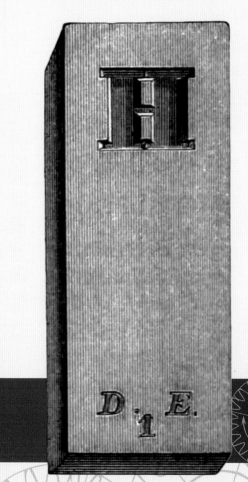

The punch, *left*, made an impression in the matrix, *right*, which would then be used to cast the metal type.

be used for any letter. The matrix was placed into the bottom of this mold and molten metal poured in. When the metal cooled and hardened, it was tapped out, producing a single piece of cast type with a metal stem for handling. Dozens of copies of that letter were cast, and then a different matrix was slipped in to the mold.

Gutenberg also had to invent a way of firmly holding the type into lines of text so the type would not shift when paper was pressed onto it. Each line of type was assembled by hand—letter by letter, space by space—on a wood or iron tray. When Gutenberg was ready to print a different page, he simply removed the type from the frame and replaced it with a new set of type.

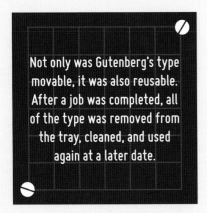

Not only was Gutenberg's type movable, it was also reusable. After a job was completed, all of the type was removed from the tray, cleaned, and used again at a later date.

Gutenberg's next challenge was developing the right mixture of metal to cast his type. He required an alloy that would melt easily, harden quickly, and be inexpensive to make. The exact composition of Gutenberg's metal mixture is unknown. However, scholars believe tin may well have been part of the alloy, and certainly lead was used. A question surrounds the frequent claim that Gutenberg used antimony, another metal, in his mixture. Analyses of other printers' type metals from the late 1400s and early 1500s confirm the presence of antimony, but historians are uncertain if Gutenberg himself used antimony.

On the Press

Wooden-screw presses had been used since the first century CE for a wide variety of purposes, including juice and oil production and to compress or smooth cloth. The Gutenberg press modified the design of a screw press and incorporated several important innovations, including a wooden box, called a hose, and a platen—a heavy, flat wooden board. When a wooden screw at the top of the press was turned, the platen came straight down, pressing the paper onto the inked type. The press also had a wooden bed on which the tray containing the type was placed. The bed was designed to slide in and out in order to position it properly under the platen.

All the finished, cast pieces of type were stored in a case called a type case, which was divided into many compartments. Each letter, number, and character had a compartment of its own. One at a time, the typesetter, or compositor, handpicked the letters he needed to spell out words and lined them up on a holder called a composing stick. The stick was a measuring tool that made each line exactly the same length. To make the spaces between

REFINING THE PRINTING PRESS

One of the goals of early printers was to improve the wooden screw that lowered and raised the platen. The first major breakthrough was the development of a metal screw by a press builder in Nuremburg, Germany, in the 1550s. The new screw was easier and smoother to turn and made the press more stable as the paper was pressed against the inked type.

The typesetter used a composing stick to space the letters and make the lines of text even.

words, he used pieces of type with no letters on them. Then he placed each line of type on the tray. Thin blank slivers of metal were inserted between the lines to create spacing. When the entire page had been composed, the tray was secured into the chase and positioned on the bed under the platen. The job was ready to be printed.

As the compositor set type in his composing stick, two workers operated the printing press. The first pressman spread an even film of ink on the type with ink balls, which Gutenberg himself designed. The balls were made of leather pads, mounted in wooden cups with handles and stuffed with wool or horsehair. The balls were covered with a piece of sheepskin. After ink was applied to the balls, the worker tapped them down onto the face of the type. Small amounts of ink were added periodically to replace what was used as work proceeded.

A second pressman placed a sheet of paper into a frame and then positioned the frame directly above the inked type. As he turned a handle attached to the wooden screw of the press, the platen lowered until it touched the back of the frame. He continued to pull the handle harder, pressing the paper more firmly against the type. He then raised the platen by reversing the direction of the screw and slid out the bed. As the freshly printed sheet was removed from the frame and hung to dry, the inker moved back into position to ink the type for the next impression.

Gutenberg's newly developed technologies remained unchanged for hundreds of years. His technique of printing, called letterpress, is still used today.

WHAT HAPPENED TO GUTENBERG?

From the mid-1450s to his death in 1468, details about Gutenberg's life are largely open to question. Printed material using his type, such as calendars and indulgences, indicate he was still at work. The types of the 36-Line Bible, printed around 1458 to 1460, are believed to be Gutenberg's. Many researchers believe the *Catholicon*, a Latin dictionary printed in Mainz in 1460, was also Gutenberg's. The book is 746 pages and set in the smallest type used to that date.[1]

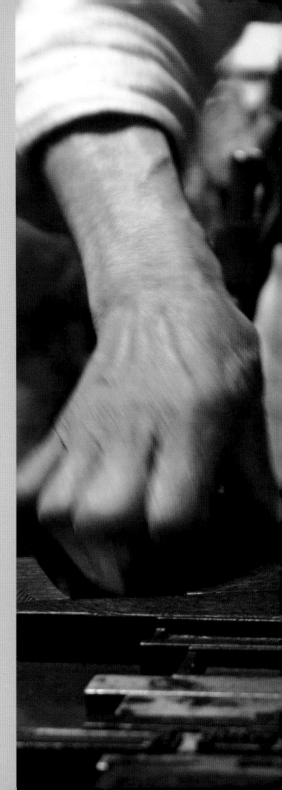

CHAPTER 5

THE PRINT
REVOLUTION

I n 1462, troops of Archbishop Adolf of Nassau conquered
Mainz in a battle over religious authority in the region. Many
printers found themselves without work and left the city to find
employment elsewhere. These skilled craftsmen were welcomed
wherever they went. By 1480, printing presses were running in
roughly 110 towns in Europe.[1] By 1500, the number of towns with
presses had more than doubled to 236.[2] Print was everywhere, and
it was here to stay.

The art and technology of printing spread quickly through Europe.

Early Years of Growth

The second half of the 1400s saw the transition from the Middle Ages to modern times in Europe. It was marked by a growing interest in science, art, and exploration, as well as increasing general knowledge about humankind and the world. Paper was in abundance, and free trade and commerce were on the rise.

The largest supporters of the new technology were clergymen. Bishops often had printers set up shops in their towns, and several monasteries even took in printers who taught monks the new art. The church also printed or paid for classical Greek and Roman works and books for general education purposes. It was also not uncommon for wealthy patrons of printers to install printing presses and pressmen in their homes, from where they published books for the educated aristocracy. In time, lawyers and government officials, as well as wealthy merchants wishing to build up their personal libraries, became buyers of books.

In 1609, the first numbered and dated newsbooks—the ancestors of our modern newspaper—were printed in Germany. Newsbooks generally contained eight to 16 pages and covered a single story or event.

Most important was the impact of the new technology on European society and culture. Many scholars believe the printing revolution had its greatest influence in four areas: language, religion, education, and politics.

Printing and Language

More than three-quarters of the books printed before 1500 were in Latin, the language of the clergy and Europe's educated classes.[3] Soon, however, the general population began to desire books in the languages they spoke in their everyday lives. Printers began producing works in the local vernacular, including English, French, Spanish, German, Italian, and Flemish.

By the end of the 1400s, printing had spread through Germany, Italy, France, Belgium, and the Netherlands until nearly every important town had a printing press. Soon, the same was true of Portugal, Spain, and Poland. By the 1500s, the printing phenomenon had reached Turkey, India, and Russia.

One of the most influential printers of the vernacular was William Caxton of England. Sometime around 1475, he printed the first book in the English language, his translation of the ancient Greek Trojan War story, *The Recuyell of Historyes of Troye*. From a small shop near Westminster Abbey in London, Caxton printed in a style of English he thought most people could read.

Printing and Religion

In medieval and early modern times, the dominant religious force in Europe was the Roman Catholic Church. Protests against abuses in the Church were common, but it wasn't until the early 1500s that the protests of one man sparked a sweeping revolution.

On March 31, 1517, Martin Luther, a Catholic priest, nailed several handwritten sheets of paper to the door of a church in Wittenberg, Germany. In this document, known as the Ninety-Five Theses, Luther stated his grievances against the Catholic church. He was outraged by the sale of indulgences, the indifference of the pope toward the poor, and other church practices.

Luther realized the power of the printing press. He published dozens of texts, sermons, fliers, pamphlets, and thousands of copies of the Theses to explain his opinions. Within a few short years, many of his works were available in several languages. The movement, called

King Edward IV of England receives a copy of a book printed by William Caxton, c. 1477.

THE KING JAMES BIBLE

In 1604, King James I of England and Scotland instructed a group of clergymen to create a new English translation of the Bible. The king's printer, Robert Barker, put out the first edition of the King James Bible in 1611. The language used in the King James Bible had a powerful influence on English-speaking cultures and literature. In England, it helped heal religious divisions and shaped that nation by bringing the words of the Bible to common people in their own language. The King James Bible has been called one of the most influential books in the history of the English-speaking world and possibly in the entire world.

ENGRAVING

In early printing, illustrations—like the words on a page—were produced with woodcut blocks. An artist cut an image into a block of wood, creating a raised surface on which ink was placed. In the early 1400s, artists began using metal to print their work. The artist engraves the lines of the drawing into a metal plate. To print with an engraved plate, the entire surface of the plate is covered with ink, which is then wiped away. Some of the ink remains in the cuts in the plate. To transfer the ink to paper, the printer uses pressure to force up the paper into the inked grooves.

the Protestant Reformation, took root in other countries, among them Switzerland, Scotland, England, Denmark, and France. By the time of Luther's death in 1546, roughly half of Germany had split from the Roman Catholic Church.

Printing and Education

In the early years of the new technology, printers often published reprints of classical literature. Between 1495 and 1498, Italian printer Aldus Manutius published a five-volume edition of the works of Aristotle in Greek. Works by Greek, Roman, and Arabic authors and thinkers were widely published.

Soon, however, the printing press became a vehicle for spreading new scientific ideas, written for the public at large. This was especially true of anatomy and the natural sciences, such as physics, astronomy, and chemistry. Illustrations appearing in printed books were a key ingredient in the appeal of scientific literature. In 1543, *On the Revolution*

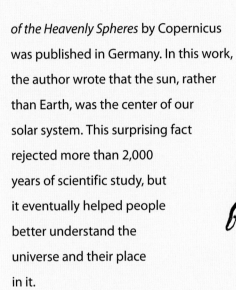

of the *Heavenly Spheres* by Copernicus
was published in Germany. In this work,
the author wrote that the sun, rather
than Earth, was the center of our
solar system. This surprising fact
rejected more than 2,000
years of scientific study, but
it eventually helped people
better understand the
universe and their place
in it.

That same year, Andreas Vesalius brought out *On the Fabric of the Human Body*, which included engravings of human anatomy featuring, for the first time, incredible images of veins, bones, tissues, and muscles. The book

Vesalius's detailed engravings revolutionized the field of medicine.

remained one of the most important works on human anatomy for decades.

Accounts of the great voyages of exploration by adventurers such as Christopher Columbus, Amerigo Vespucci, Hernán Cortés, and others in the 1500s were widely printed in numerous languages. Before 1550, only 83 books on geography were published in France. In the next 60 years, nearly 450 geographic works were published there.[4]

Printing and Politics

Europe's royalty was quick to recognize how the power of the press could influence political thinking. One of the most powerful political works of the 1500s was Niccolò Machiavelli's *The Prince*, written in Italian. Published in 1532, the book is a study of how to acquire and maintain political power.

Printed maps shared new geographic knowledge from Europe's voyages of discovery during the 1500s.

By the end of the 1500s, the printing press had conquered most of the Old World. Its next greatest impact would be felt in the Americas, where it would help put a new nation on a path toward democracy.

THE PRINTING PRESS
SPREADS

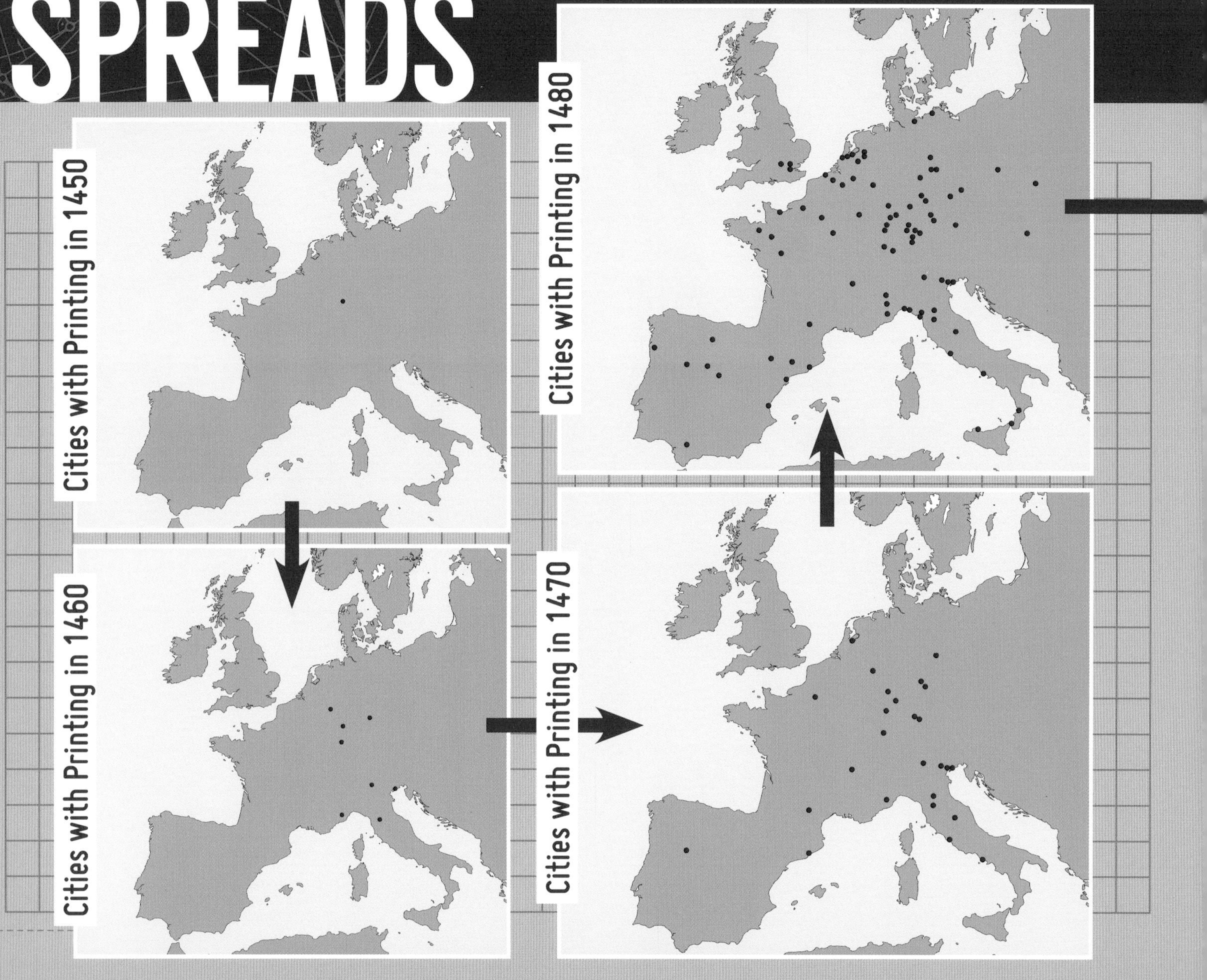

Cities with Printing in 1450

Cities with Printing in 1460

Cities with Printing in 1470

Cities with Printing in 1480

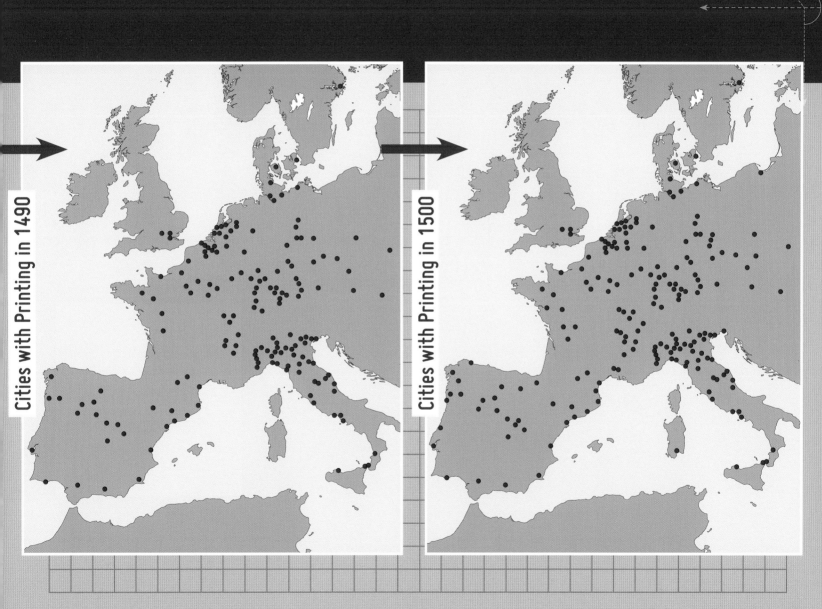

Cities with Printing in 1490

Cities with Printing in 1500

CHAPTER 6

EARLY AMERICAN PRINTING

The English settlers who sailed across the Atlantic Ocean to found a colony in Massachusetts in the early 1600s brought with them a few religious texts and other printed material. They quickly set about establishing schools and a printing press.

In 1638, settlers built a college in Cambridge, Massachusetts, which later came to be known as Harvard University. Later that year, or perhaps in 1639, Elizabeth Glover, the wife of the deceased Reverend Jose Glover, established a printing press on the grounds of the college. It had been her husband's plan to set up a press when he arrived in America from England, but Jose died on the

Benjamin Franklin is one of the most famous early American printers.

voyage, leaving Elizabeth to finish his work. She hired Stephen Day, a locksmith, to set up the press and run it. His 18-year-old son, Matthew, assisted him.

In 1640, Day and Elizabeth printed the first book in the English colonies, the *Bay Psalm Book*, a translation of the Psalms from Hebrew into English. For 40 years, the press in Cambridge produced the only printed material in the colonies. Its works included the Eliot Indian Bible, a translation of the entire Bible into the local Algonquin language, printed in 1661.

In time, presses were established throughout New England and the middle and southern colonies. By 1763, printing presses were running in all the original 13 colonies.

Day's printing press was later moved to Vermont and today is part of the collections of the Vermont Historical Society.

The Nature of Early American Printing

In the English colonies throughout the 1600s and 1700s, printing equipment was very similar to the equipment European printers used at the end of the 1400s. But American printers did not cast their own type and often lacked the tools to run an efficient printing operation. It wasn't until 1769 that the first type designed and cast in America was produced. Colonial printers generally bought their presses from England, but by the mid-1770s, a few American manufacturers began building presses and other printing equipment.

America gradually came to produce printing supplies as well. In 1690, William Bradford, the first printer in Philadelphia, established the first American paper mill with William Rittenhouse near Germantown, Pennsylvania. At first, American printers imported ready-to-use ink from English manufacturers. By the 1720s, however, many printers began to mix inks in their shops.

Many print shops were family-run businesses operated by the printer, his wife, and his children. Printers often took on apprentices who worked without pay in return for room and board and training in the art of printing.

In colonial times, newspapers, legal forms, almanacs, and primers, which taught reading and writing, were the principal printed matter. Legal handbooks for lawyers and government officials were common. Legal guides for the common people, such as *Every Man His Own Lawyer* and *An Essay of Crimes and Punishments*, were also popular.

Colonial Women Printers

Women printers played a key role in developing new technology in the colonies. Dinah Nuthead of Saint Mary's City, Maryland, was the first woman to be licensed to print in America. She took over her husband's printing operation after his death in 1695, printing government forms.

Also in Maryland, in 1738 Anne Catherine Green married Jonas Green, the printer of the *Maryland Gazette*. After her husband's death in 1767, Anne assumed control of the printing business and inherited Jonas's position as official printer of the colony.

In Rhode Island, Ann Franklin, widow of James and sister-in-law of Benjamin Franklin, ran the family's printing business after James's death in 1735. Ann printed pamphlets and material for the colony for the next 28 years until her death.

Colonial Newspapers and Censorship

By the late 1700s, newspapers had become a principal feature of colonial publishing. From the time the first newspaper appeared in 1690 until 1775, 78 different newspapers were published in the colonies.[1] By the year 1820, more than 2,000 newspapers had been published in the colonies and then in the states.[2]

Reporting news of the outside world and informing readers about local events was often a one-person operation. The printer-writer not only printed the news but also gathered the news and wrote it. Many printer-journalists used their newspapers to shape public opinion. It didn't take long before such freedom of opinion thrust publishers into conflict with local authorities.

On September 25, 1690, Benjamin Harris of Boston printed *Publick Occurrences*, the first newspaper in the colonies. Four days later, government officials in Massachusetts shut down the paper. They seized copies of the publication and burned them. Harris was warned never to publish the paper again. The authorities claimed they acted because the newspaper was printed without permission and it contained inaccurate reports. With its actions, the government struck fear into the hearts of potential newspaper publishers. Boston did not have another newspaper until April 1704,

> "Maroon two Americans on a desert island, it has been said, and before the next sunset one of them will have started a newspaper."[3]
>
> —John Winterich, *Early American Books and Printing*

when John Campbell published the first issue of the *Boston News-Letter*.

Harris wasn't the first—or last—case of press censorship in the colonies. In 1682, William Nuthead of Virginia was prevented from printing the proceedings of the colony's assembly without permission. Printing was then outlawed in Virginia. Nuthead moved his press to Maryland, where he printed attacks on the Catholic-led government there. His wife, Dinah, took over the business

when he died. In 1693, the Quaker government of Philadelphia charged William Bradford with printing inflammatory anti-Quaker material. Bradford was jailed, and authorities seized his press and equipment.

On November 5, 1733, John Peter Zenger of New York began publishing the *New-York Weekly Journal*. Zenger published a series of articles that were critical of the colonial governor, William Cosby. In November 1734, Zenger was arrested and imprisoned on a charge of libel against Governor Cosby. At the trial in 1735, the jury found Zenger not guilty. The decision was a monumental victory for the freedom of the press in America.

The Franklin Family

One of the most prominent colonial printers was James Franklin, the older brother of Benjamin Franklin. After arriving from London in 1717, James established a printing business in Boston. In 1721, he began publishing Boston's third newspaper, the *New England Courant*, in which Franklin criticized members of the clergy and influential men in the government. Within a year, Franklin was imprisoned by the government for four weeks for publishing libelous material. After his release from jail, Franklin resumed publishing the *Courant* and continued his attacks.

> Freedom of the press in the United States is protected by the First Amendment to the Constitution. The same clause also guarantees freedom of religion and freedom of speech.

" It is now forty years (1785) since I worked, like you, at this press, a journeyman printer."

Franklin

BENJAMIN FRANKLIN: THE PRINTING OFFICE IN WHICH HE WORKED; AND THE HOUSE WHEREIN HE RESIDED WHEN AGENT FOR PENNSYLVANIA.

Benjamin Franklin's Philadelphia home and printing press

Boston authorities responded by strictly forbidding Franklin from printing the *Courant*, or any other material, without official approval. Rather than risk further punishment, James turned over control of the *Courant* to his 17-year-old brother, Benjamin, who was then James's apprentice. The younger Franklin published the paper for a short time, but he soon headed to Philadelphia, where he worked at a weekly newspaper. In 1729, Benjamin became the publisher of the *Pennsylvania Gazette*, with which he maintained a working relationship for several decades.

During these years, Benjamin Franklin wrote and published *Poor Richard's Almanack*, a yearly pamphlet that appeared from 1732 to 1758. Written under the name "Poor Richard" or "Richard Saunders," the *Almanack* offered folksy common sense, calendars, annual weather forecasts, astrological information, and amusing verses, poems, and sayings. The almanacs sold well, providing Franklin with enough money to enable him to devote time to inventing and politics.

Seeds of Discontent

Spurred by the growth of public education, literacy in the colonies soared. Among white men in New England, for example, literacy increased from 60 percent between 1650 and 1670 to 85 percent between 1758 and 1762, and to 90 percent between 1787 and 1795.[4]

As relations with England grew tenser during the 1700s, a storm of political writing appeared in the colonies. One of the most influential writers of the American Revolution was British-born Thomas Paine, who came to America in 1774. Within a few months of his arrival, Paine had become a writer and the editor of the *Pennsylvania Magazine*. In January 1776, Paine published the pamphlet *Common Sense*. Printed by Robert Bell of Philadelphia, it sold several hundred thousand copies in

ISAIAH THOMAS: JACK OF ALL TRADES

Boston-born Isaiah Thomas was one of the first major figures in American printing. During a career that began at age seven setting type, Thomas emerged as a leading colonial printer, papermaker, publisher, and bookseller. In 1770, he started a newspaper called the *Massachusetts Spy*, which soon became the best-selling paper in New England. The *Spy* was an important source of news for the patriot cause. When paper became nearly impossible to obtain during the Revolutionary War, Thomas reduced the number of pages in each edition and continued publishing. After the war, Thomas built a large, successful publishing program that included history, music, almanacs, children's books, spelling books, and medical and scientific books.

REVOLUTION AND PROPAGANDA

On the night of March 5, 1770, in Boston, a crowd of Americans began hurling snowballs and rocks at a group of British soldiers occupying the town. A shot rang out from a British musket, and several soldiers fired their weapons. When the smoke cleared, five civilians lay dead on the street. Three weeks later, printed illustrations entitled "The Bloody Massacre in King-Street" were offered for sale in Boston newspapers. Paul Revere, a metalworker and engraver, created the print that depicted the event, which eventually became known as the Boston Massacre. Thousands of copies of the print were sold throughout the colonies, fueling anti-British sentiment. It was a very effective piece of war propaganda.

the next few years. It was widely distributed in England and translated into several foreign languages. Paine's superbly written, direct argument for independence established him as the most convincing writer of the revolution.

Opposition to pro-independence writers and publishers, however, was strong and loud. Loyalists—pro-British Americans who rejected breaking ties with England—also used the press to voice their opinions. Loyalist newspapers operated in ten towns occupied by British forces. Dozens of loyalist writers sharply criticized colonial society and the patriot demand for independence.

Paul Revere's engraving of the Boston Massacre fanned rebellion in the colonies and proved the power of the press.

BUTCHER'S HALL

Engrav'd Printed & Sold by PAUL REVERE BOSTON

Unhappy BOSTON! see thy Sons deplore,
Thy hallow'd Walks besmear'd with guiltless Gore:
While faithless P—n and his savage Bands,
With murd'rous Rancour stretch their bloody Hands;
Like fierce Barbarians grinning o'er their Prey,
Approve the Carnage and enjoy the Day.

If scalding drops from Rage from Anguish Wrung,
If speechless Sorrows lab'ring for a Tongue,
Or if a weeping World can ought appease
The plaintive Ghosts of Victims such as these:
The Patriot's copious Tears for each are shed,
A glorious Tribute which embalms the Dead.

But know, FATE summons to that awful Goal,
Where JUSTICE strips the Murd'rer of his Soul:
Should venal C—ts the scandal of the Land,
Snatch the relentless Villain from her Hand,
Keen Execrations on this Plate inscrib'd,
Shall reach a JUDGE who never can be brib'd.

The unhappy Sufferers were Mess.rs Sam.l Gray Sam.l Maverick, Jam.s Caldwell, Crispus Attucks & Pat.k Carr

Killed. Six wounded; two of them (Christr Monk & John Clark) Mortally

Published in 1770 by Paul Revere Boston

CHAPTER 7

THE AGE OF
REASON

Beginning in the late 1600s, remarkable cultural changes swept across Europe. In the period known as the Enlightenment, European writers, scientists, and thinkers examined the world, using reason and intellect rather than religious belief. Enlightenment thinkers believed advances in science and technology would transform society and spur a new age of equality and progress for mankind. The movement spread throughout Europe and to the United States, continuing to the end of the 1700s. "Print," wrote Roy Porter in *The Creation of the Modern World*, "proved the great engine for the spread of enlightened views and values."[1]

Effig
Ex Archetypo. q

Iohannis Locke

...sao Alexandri Geekie Chirurgi adservatur expressa.

THE
WORKS
OF
JOHN LOCKE, Esq;

In Three Volumes.

The CONTENTS of which follow in the next Leaf.

With ALPHABETICAL TABLES.

VOL. I.

The FOURTH EDITION.

John Locke's writings were a key catalyst of the Enlightenment.

LONDON,

Printed for EDMUND PARKER, at the Bible and Crown, in Lombard-Street; EDWARD SYMON, against the Royal-Exchange, in Cornhill; CHARLES HITCH, at the Red Lion in Pater...

The Birth of the Enlightenment

The Enlightenment had its roots in England, beginning with the publication of John Locke's *An Essay Concerning Human Understanding* in 1690. Locke writes that the human mind starts as a blank slate, or *tabula rasa*. All ideas are formed by experience. In other writings, Locke claims all people have the basic rights to life, to own property, and to revolt against corrupt governments. Locke's ideas were adapted by the Founding Fathers of the United States and incorporated into the Declaration of Independence.

The Enlightenment fanned out across Europe. In Germany, philosopher Immanuel Kant wrote about the relationship of mind and matter. His most famous work was the *Critique of Pure Reason*, published in 1781. In Italy, Cesare Beccaria published *On Crimes and Punishment* in 1764. The book condemned torture and was instrumental in abolishing the death penalty in Italy. Beccaria believed the role of government was to achieve the greatest good for the greatest number of people. This concept deeply influenced American thinkers such as Thomas Jefferson and John Adams.

The Enlightenment in Great Britain

In 1707, Scotland and England joined to form the kingdom of Great Britain. Scotland's union with its wealthier, more populous neighbor greatly boosted its economic and intellectual development. By the 1750s, Scotland, particularly Edinburgh, supported a thriving intellectual community, with universities, libraries, newspapers, and societies dedicated to the advancement of knowledge in numerous fields.

The English Enlightenment was fueled by increased literacy and a dramatic surge in the number of books printed in London. In about 1720, roughly 21,000 titles were published. By 1790, the number reached approximately 56,000 titles.[2] Notable titles printed during this time include Jonathan Swift's *Gulliver's Travels* (1726), Laurence Sterne's *Tristram Shandy* (1759), and Edward Gibbon's monumental *History of the Decline and Fall of the Roman Empire,* published in six volumes between 1776 and 1778.

Among the leading thinkers of the Enlightenment were Sir Isaac Newton and Mary Wollstonecraft. Newton was a physicist and mathematician who developed the law of gravity and three fundamental laws of motion. His

Isaac Newton changed the way science is practiced and understood.

groundbreaking theory about planets and heavenly bodies changed the way people viewed the universe. The first edition of his most important work, *Philosophiæ Naturalis Principia Mathematica,* was published in Latin in 1687. Subsequent editions were released in 1713 and 1726.

Mary Wollstonecraft, born in London, was an early spokesperson for women's rights. In *A Vindication of the Rights of Woman*, published in 1792, she writes that the English educational system intentionally trained women to be incompetent. Wollstonecraft argues that a system more equal to the boys' educational system would produce women who could be capable workers in many professions. Her writings profoundly influenced later American women's rights advocates such as Margaret Fuller and Elizabeth Cady Stanton.

Adam Smith's *Inquiry into the Nature and Causes of the Wealth of Nations* (1776) established him as the most influential thinker in the development of modern economic theory. In it, the Scotland-born Smith argued against government interference in the economy. Instead, he believed an "invisible hand" would guide it, a theory that established the groundwork for modern capitalism.

Newspapers, too, thrived throughout the 1700s. Between 1690 and 1780, the number of newspapers printed in England each year rose from less than 1 million to 14 million.[3] London was the hub of the newspaper industry. In 1712, the city had 12 newspapers, and by 1811, there were 52.[4]

The first daily newspaper in England appeared in 1702. It was published by Elizabeth Mallet, who had taken over her husband's printing business when he died in 1683.

The French Enlightenment

Although the Enlightenment had its roots in England, the movement truly blossomed in France. Thinkers demanded reforms in the church and its traditions and criticized the rule of French monarchies. In the *Spirit of the Laws* (1748), Baron de Montesquieu expanded on the ideas of John Locke and emphasized the importance of a separation of powers in government. His proposed system of checks and balances was the model America's Founding Fathers adapted roughly 35 years later.

Government tyranny and the rights of the people were often the subjects of two of France's greatest writers: Voltaire and Jean-Jacques Rousseau. Voltaire used wit and satire to speak out against tyranny and bigotry. In *Candide* (1759), his most famous novel, Voltaire attacks the hypocrisy of the church and the corrupting power of money.

In *The Social Contract* (1762), Jean-Jacques Rousseau writes, "man is born free, and everywhere he is in chains."[5] Rousseau rejects the idea that monarchs were empowered by God to rule. Only the people have that right—and no laws are valid unless agreed upon by the people. This idea provided the spark that brought on the French Revolution three decades later.

Printing and Human Liberty

Thanks to a vibrant book trade with Great Britain, American colonists became acquainted with the progressive thinking of 1700s Europe. Sir William Blackstone's *Commentaries on the Laws of England* (1765–1769) became the basis of law school education in America. The political thought expressed by Scottish historian David Hume in works such as *A Treatise of Human Nature* (1739) and *Essays, Moral and Political* (1758) are believed to have had a strong influence on James Madison and the US Constitution. *The Law of Nations*, written by Swiss philosopher Emmerich de Vattel, outlined the principles by which governments should interact. George Washington and Benjamin Franklin both had copies in their personal libraries.

Eighteenth-century printers at work, as illustrated in *Encyclopédie* by Denis Diderot

ENCYCLOPÉDIE

One of the greatest printing achievements of the French Enlightenment was the production of *Encyclopédie*, a massive encyclopedia compiled and printed in Paris. Philosopher-translator Denis Diderot and mathematician Jean d'Alembert supervised the project. Between 1751 and 1772, 17 volumes of text and 11 volumes of beautifully illustrated plates were published.[6] The work includes approximately 70,000 articles on subjects ranging from African trade to zoology. More than 140 people contributed articles, among them Voltaire, Jean-Jacques Rousseau, Montesquieu, and Diderot and d'Alembert themselves.[7] By 1789, approximately 25,000 copies of *Encyclopédie* had been distributed around the world.[8]

By the 1800s, the printing press had become a powerful tool in the fight for human freedom. In Great Britain, William Wilberforce, a member of the House of Commons, worked tirelessly to end slavery. In 1807, he published *A Letter on the Abolition of the Slave Trade.* The book was printed by Luke Hansard, the official printer of the *Journals of the House of Commons.* In March 1807, a bill to abolish the slave trade in the West Indies was carried into law.

In the United States, abolitionists also used the power of print to break the bonds of slavery. William Lloyd Garrison, a printer-journalist born in Massachusetts, began publishing the antislavery newspaper the *Liberator* on January 1, 1831. The paper circulated both in the United States and Great Britain, providing an important source of antislavery information. The *Liberator* was published each week—without missing a single issue—for 35 years. Garrison published its last edition in December 1865 when the Thirteenth Amendment to the US Constitution abolished slavery in the United States.

The *Liberator* was only one of many publications that fought to end slavery. Harriet Beecher Stowe's *Uncle Tom's Cabin*, published in 1852, depicts the cruelty and brutality of slavery. The book quickly sold more than 3 million copies.[9] The *Slave's Friend*, published 1835–1839, was an antislavery magazine for children.

Print Technology Marches On

The arrival of the Industrial Revolution in the second half of the 1800s brought sweeping changes to the technology of print. As the iron industry developed, methods of making and shaping metals improved. In 1772, Wilhelm Haas of

Basel, Switzerland, developed iron replacements for the parts of the wooden press that experienced the greatest stress. In 1790, William Nicholson was awarded a patent for a design that replaced the flat platen with a three-sided cylinder. A separate sheet of paper was placed on each side of the cylinder. The cylinder moved up and down, pressing the paper against the type. After one sheet was printed, the cylinder rotated and a second sheet of paper was positioned above the type. Nicholson was unable to build a working model, however. In 1800, Englishman Charles Stanhope designed a press made entirely of iron, including all the working parts and its frame.

At about the same time, in 1796, Alois Senefelder, a German playwright, devised a way of transferring ink onto paper using a flat printing plate. His invention, called lithography, eventually made movable type nearly obsolete. Based on the principle that grease and water do not mix, Senefelder drew on a flat piece of limestone with a greasy crayon. Then he dampened the stone with water. As he suspected, the water stuck only to those areas of the stone that were not covered by the greasy design.

BOOKS ON THE FRONTIER

During the settling of the American West in the 1700s and 1800s, people on the frontier were eager for reading material. Books were the main carriers of knowledge and culture to new settlements. Frontier printers set up small shops in towns, publishing newspapers, law books, schoolbooks, almanacs, and works of local interest. A favorite among frontier printers was a small, portable wooden press developed by Scottish immigrant Adam Ramage in Philadelphia. Once a region became accessible by trail routes or waterways, new and used books were imported in great quantities from the East.

Then he covered the stone's surface with ink, and the ink stuck only to the greasy design. When he pressed a sheet of paper against the stone, the ink on the greasy area transferred to the paper. It would take many years, however, for Senefelder's idea to be further developed and put into widespread use.

Friedrich Koenig of Suhl, Germany, began working on a steam-powered cylinder press in 1802. In 1812, Koenig produced a press capable of printing 400 sheets per hour.[10] The *London Times* commissioned Koenig to build two double-cylinder, steam-powered presses. Each was capable of producing 1,100 pages an hour.[11] In November 1814, the presses began printing the *Times*.

In lithography, the oil-based ink sticks only to the artist's design, allowing a print to be transferred to paper.

CHAPTER 8

TECHNOLOGY MOVES
FORWARD

B y the middle of the 1800s, important developments were revolutionizing print production. New inventions included improvements in the press, mechanized typesetting, and other groundbreaking technologies.

In 1844, American printer Richard Hoe invented the Type Revolving Machine, a rotary printing press that was a variation on Koenig's cylinder press. Instead of placing the cast metal type on a flat bed and bringing the cylinder into contact with it, Hoe attached the type around a 6.5-foot (2 m) horizontal cylinder itself. He also made the cylinder round, rather than using Koenig's three-sided

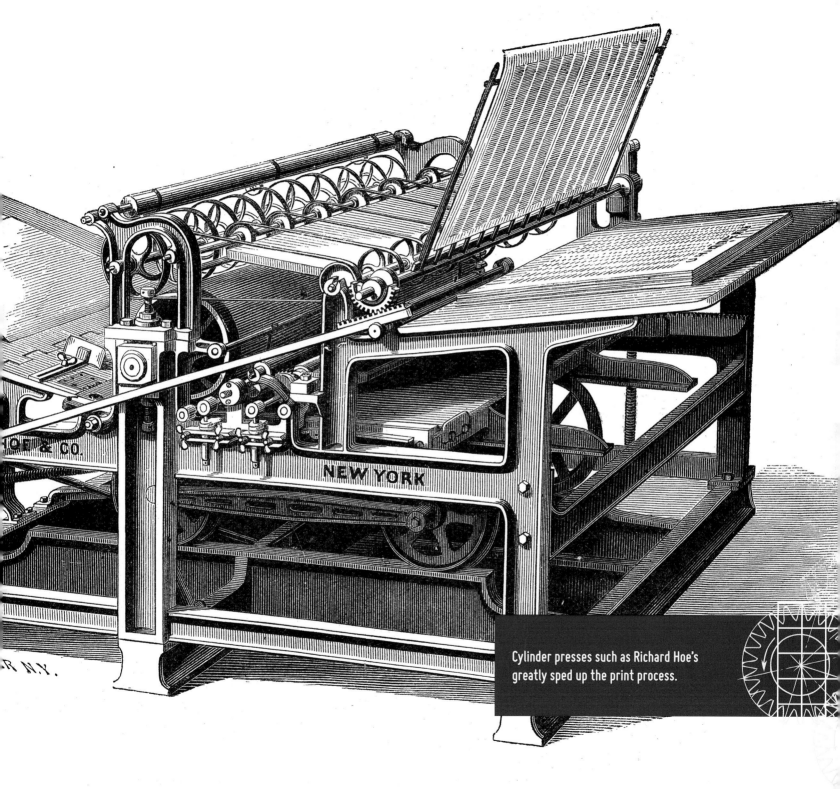

Cylinder presses such as Richard Hoe's greatly sped up the print process.

THE WEB PRESS

In 1865, William Bullock designed a new kind of rotary press, the web press. Combining Hoe's cylinder press and a new papermaking machine developed by Louis Robert in France, Bullock made the fastest printing press in the world. Robert's machine required a continuous roll of paper instead of standard single sheets. The roll of paper was called a web. In Bullock's design, the web of paper was fed into the press and cut into sheets before reaching the first of two sets of printing cylinders. Each set printed one side of the sheet.

version. The type on the cylinder transferred ink onto sheets of paper that ran under the type. In 1847, he installed the first of the Hoe Type Revolving Machines at the Philadelphia *Public Ledger*.

Photoengraving

For centuries, engraved metal plates had been used to print art. Engraving into a plate of metal by hand with a sharp tool was laborious and time-consuming. The invention of photography in 1839, however, gave printers a new idea: What if they could make a printing plate using photography?

In 1852, photographer William Henry Fox Talbot of Great Britain discovered a way to do it. Talbot coated a metal plate with a light-sensitive, acid-resistant gelatin and placed it in his camera. Then he positioned a piece of gauze mesh between his camera and an object. When he snapped a photo of the object, the mesh broke the light reflected from the object into a pattern of dots called a halftone. The light hit the gelatin coating on the plate, dissolving it into the same pattern of dots. Talbot washed the plate with another acid, which ate away the metal, leaving a surface of raised dots of different sizes. The process became known as photoengraving. Not only could it reproduce images, but a printed page of text could be photographed and made into a plate as well.

Mechanized Typesetting

For more than 400 years, printers set cast type by hand, a tedious, time-consuming task for even the most skilled type compositor. Late in the 1800s, however, two composing machines—the Linotype and the Monotype—ushered in mechanized typesetting, greatly speeding up the process of setting cast-metal type.

In 1884, Ottmar Mergenthaler of Baltimore, Maryland, introduced the Linotype machine, which, as its name implies, molds lines of type ready for printing. A single operator used a keyboard to select letter and number matrices from a chamber in the machine. This formed a line of type matrix, into which molten metal was poured. The cooled, hardened metal type was called a slug. The slugs were put into the form, which held all the type for the page to be printed. After the slugs had been used, they were automatically melted down and fed back into the machine to be used again. The matrices were carried back to their chamber, where they were automatically sorted for reuse.

LARGE LINOTYPES

By 1916, there were approximately 33,000 Linotype machines in use around the world.[1] The biggest was the Blue Streak Model 36. It stood nearly 6.5 feet (2 m) high and weighed a whopping 7,090 pounds (3,215 kg)—more than 3.5 short tons (3.2 metric tons)![2]

The linotype machine included a keyboard where the compositor typed the desired letters and numbers.

Meanwhile, another American, Tolbert Lanston, developed a technique in which punched paper tape could be used to select matrices to cast type. The setup consisted of two machines, a composer and a caster/typesetter. Each machine required an operator. One operator sat at the composer keyboard and typed out the characters to be set. The keyboard punched holes in a paper tape, with a different pattern of holes for each character. The tape was put into the caster/typesetter machine, which selected each character based on the pattern of holes in the tape, cast the type, and set it in lines.

Evolving Photographic Techniques

In 1904, Ira W. Rubel, an American, invented a new printing process that combined William Talbot's photoengraving technique and Alois Senefelder's lithography process. The new process was called offset printing. This process operates on the idea that grease and water do not mix. The photoengraved printing plate never touches the paper.

First, a photoengraved plate is treated with chemicals so inked areas will hold greasy ink but not water. The photoengraved plate is then attached to a cylinder. As the cylinder turns, the plate first passes under wet water rollers and then under another roller that carries greasy ink. As the cylinder rotates, it presses the plate against a rubber "blanket" covering another cylinder, called the offset cylinder. The ink is transferred, or offset, to the blanket, which then transfers it to paper. The paper is pressed against the offset cylinder by the impression cylinder below. The soft, smooth surface of the blanket produces a sharp, clean image.

Even with the development of photoengraving and offset printing, raised metal type was still necessary to create the original typeset page. With Thomas Edison's invention of a commercially viable light bulb in 1879, inventors had the constant, reliable light source they needed to develop a machine that could set type photographically. In phototypesetting, light passes through a disk that has letters, numbers, and other characters punched into it like a stencil. The light goes through the disk and then through a lens that focuses the light on a mirror. The mirror reflects

OFFSET PRINTING PROCESS

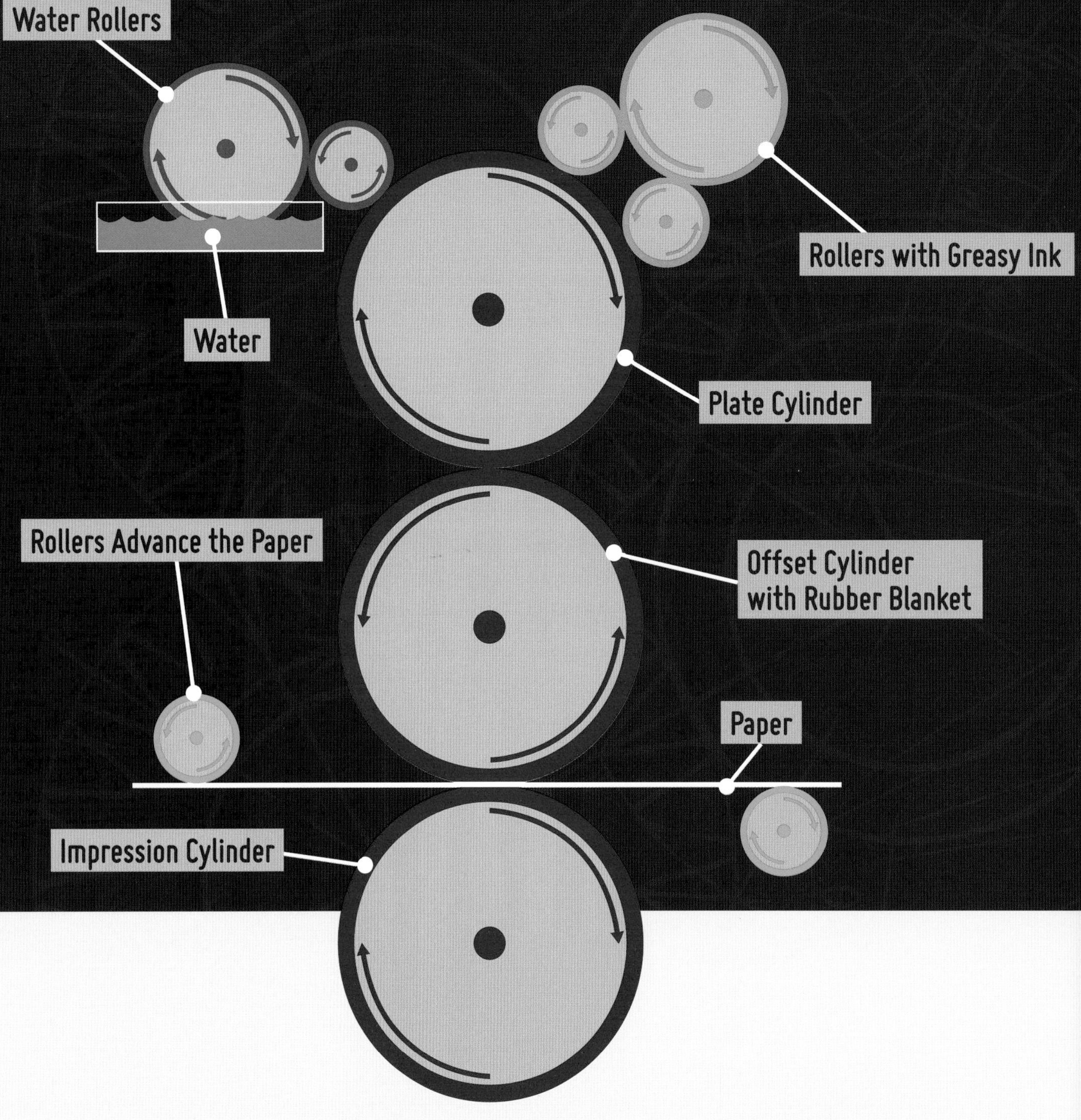

Water Rollers

Water

Rollers with Greasy Ink

Plate Cylinder

Rollers Advance the Paper

Offset Cylinder
with Rubber Blanket

Paper

Impression Cylinder

the light onto photographic paper, which causes the shape of the characters to be exposed onto the film. The film is then used to make a printing plate. The Intertype Fotosetter, introduced in 1950, was the first phototypesetting machine. It was followed by the British Monophoto in 1954.

Electrostatic Printing

During the 1940s and 1950s, the Xerox Corporation developed the copying machine, or copier, which was based on a 1938 invention by American scientist Chester F. Carlson. The copier works on the principle that opposite electrical charges attract. A drum in the machine called the photoconductor is charged with positive electricity. When the drum is exposed to light, it loses its charge. To make a copy, an original is placed on the copier's glass surface and exposed to light. The light reflects off the white areas of the original and strikes the drum below, making the drum lose its charge in only the white areas.

Meanwhile, the dark areas on the original do not reflect light onto the drum. This allows areas of positive charges to remain on the drum. Negatively charged toner, a powder used in printers, is then spread over the drum's surface, and the toner sticks to the positive charges that remain. A positively charged sheet of paper is then passed over the drum, attracting the toner away from it. The paper is heated and pressed to fuse the toner to the paper's surface, creating a copied image. The first Xerox copying machine was made commercially available in the late 1950s.

CHAPTER 9

THE DIGITAL AGE

Perhaps the most dramatic innovation in the world of printing in the last century was the computer, which entered the printing industry in the 1960s. Desktop publishing with a personal computer became possible in the 1980s. It allows users to combine text, images, charts, and other graphic elements into an electronic file. The file can be printed, or output, on a small laser printer at home or on a massive press at a commercial printing plant. Today, computers are the lifeblood of the printing industry.

Modern printing happens at high speeds on large machines using digital files.

Inkjet Printing and Laser Printing

Computers allow text and images to be digitized, broken into a pattern of dots, and stored in the computer's memory. A process was needed to transfer ink to a page without using an inked surface. One solution is to connect the computer to a printer that has a set of small nozzles. The computer instructs the printer to spray out dots of ink from the nozzles that match the pattern stored in the computer's memory. This process, called inkjet printing, is commonly used in homes and small businesses.

Laser printers, like Xerox copiers, work on the principle that opposite electric charges attract. Information from a computer is sent to the printer, and the photoreceptor drum in the printer is given a positive charge. Next, in a process called exposure, a laser light re-creates the image on the drum. In the areas exposed to the laser beam, positive charges are erased, creating an area of negative charges instead.

As the drum rotates, positively charged ink particles are transferred to the drum and stick to the parts that have a negative charge. A positively charged sheet of paper passes near the drum and attracts the negatively charged ink particles, transferring the image to the paper. The paper passes through hot rollers that fuse the ink particles to the paper. The drum is cleaned of ink and the process starts over.

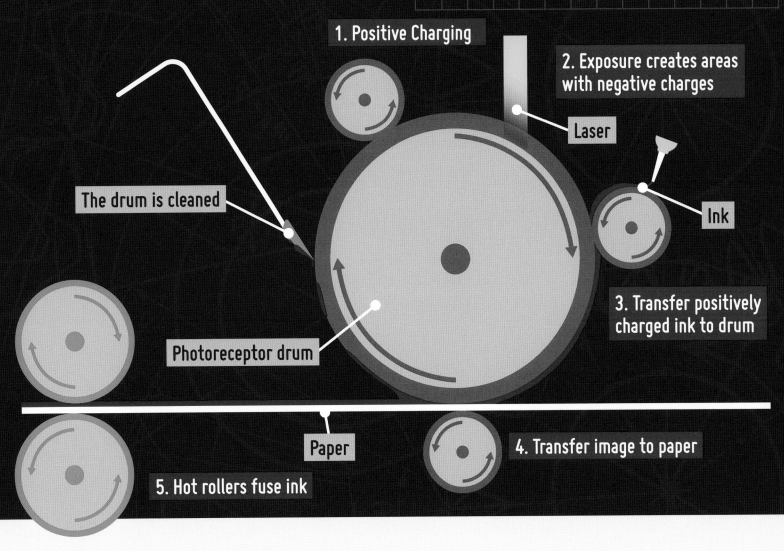

1. Positive Charging

2. Exposure creates areas with negative charges

Laser

Ink

The drum is cleaned

3. Transfer positively charged ink to drum

Photoreceptor drum

Paper

4. Transfer image to paper

5. Hot rollers fuse ink

Faster, Better, Cheaper

Computers came into use in printing in the 1960s, allowing electronic typesetting and book production. They provide the basis for two of the most widely used processes in print technology today: computer to film printing (CTF) and computer to plate printing (CTP).

In CTF, information stored in a computer—anything from a simple page of text or a single image to digital files containing all the visual elements of a large book—is output directly to film. The film is transferred onto a lithographic plate and put on an offset printing press.

In the newer technology, CTP, a computer's digital information is output directly to a printing plate. Because CTP eliminates the step of transferring the film image to the printing plate, it produces sharper, more detailed results.

GOOGLE BOOKS

Internet search company Google developed a service that allows people to search and browse books online from the comfort of their home or office. Publishers, authors, and libraries provide books and magazines to Google, which scans and digitizes the material and stores it in a digital database. You can search Google Books in the same way you would do any web search. On the books.google.com site, type in the name of the book you're looking for or a topic you want to check out, and you'll receive a list of appropriate matches. Each match provides important information about the book, such as title, author, and date of publication. Some books provide you with a few pages from the book as a limited preview. Older books in which the owner's copyright has expired can often be downloaded, saved, or printed. In 2013, the database included more than 30 million titles.[2]

The Electronic Book

An electronic book, or e-book, is a digital file containing text and images that can be displayed on a computer screen or other electronic device or e-reader, such as a Kindle, Nook, Kobo, or iPad. Many e-books are digital versions of printed books, including novels, schoolbooks, do-it-yourself manuals, magazines, and even comic books. E-books are available on the Internet as files that can be downloaded and read on a device or as Web pages that can only be read online.

Many e-books are produced and sold at the same time as the printed version of the book or magazine. Some e-books are put on sale after the print version is released. In recent years, publishers sometimes sell only the electronic

Digital and print media continue to exist side by side.

version of a book. However, it's not even necessary to buy an e-book to enjoy their benefits. There are millions of free e-books available online at dozens of different websites.

A Return to a World without Print?

The digital age is changing the way we get data. Computer networks, the Internet, and e-books provide access to a nearly endless amount of data. Do these remarkable technologies signal the end of the printed page?

It's not likely books will disappear anytime in the near future. In the United States alone, approximately 2.5 billion books are sold each year.[3] In addition, a Pew Poll conducted in 2014 revealed that roughly 70 percent of American adults read at least one print book each year.[4] And print isn't only about books. Imagine a supermarket without signs or a restaurant without menus. The printed word is everywhere in our society.

And Gutenberg's contribution is not forgotten. One of the most memorable tributes to Johann Gutenberg was written April 7, 1900, by Mark Twain, the author of *The Adventures of Tom Sawyer* and *Adventures of Huckleberry Finn*. In a letter celebrating the opening of the Gutenberg Museum in Mainz, Germany, Twain wrote:

All the world acknowledges that the invention of Gutenberg is the greatest event that secular history has recorded. Gutenberg's achievement created a new and wonderful earth. . . . During the past 500 years Gutenberg's invention . . . found truth astir on earth and gave it wings. . . . Science was found lurking in corners, much prosecuted; Gutenberg's invention gave it freedom on land and sea and brought it within reach of every mortal. Arts and industries, badly handicapped, received new life.[5]

From its earliest, humble beginnings in Germany more than 550 years ago to the high-speed presses of today, the printing press has shaped—and continues to reshape—our world.

After years of explosive growth, the sale of e-books is slowing down. Print books dominate the market. In the first half of 2014, sales of print books accounted for two-thirds of all book sales in the United States.[6]

THE NEXT GENERATION: PRINTING ON DEMAND

Today's high-speed offset printing presses can churn out thousands of copies of a book or magazine in only minutes. The four-story-tall DIAMONDSTAR printing press, for example, can print 90,000 full-color, 96-page newspapers in an hour.[7] Offset printing is speedy, but the cost of preparing plates for every page to be printed can be costly. This means publishers have to print lots of copies of a book, usually 1,000 or more, to reduce the cost per copy.

But what can a publishing company do if it wants to print fewer than 1,000 copies of a book? The answer is print on demand (POD). POD is printing only when there is a demand for the book. Suppose a publisher merely wants to get an idea of how a book might sell in a certain region. Or if the publisher wanted only enough copies to send to book critics and reviewers? It wouldn't make sense to print thousands and thousands of copies of a book. That would waste money, and the unused copies would end up sitting in a warehouse gathering dust.

With POD printing, you can print one copy or many hundreds of copies. The printing is done directly from text and image files created and stored on computers. The printing machines are relatively small units, but they can provide high-quality printed books equal to those created by huge offset presses. The cost per book of POD printing is higher than printing thousands of copies with offset. However, by printing small quantities of books, publishers do not run the risk of getting stuck with unsold books.

POD also allows anyone to create books to sell or give as gifts. Many people use POD to print books of family recipes, photo albums, poetry, and even novels and nonfiction books. With POD, everyone can be a publisher!

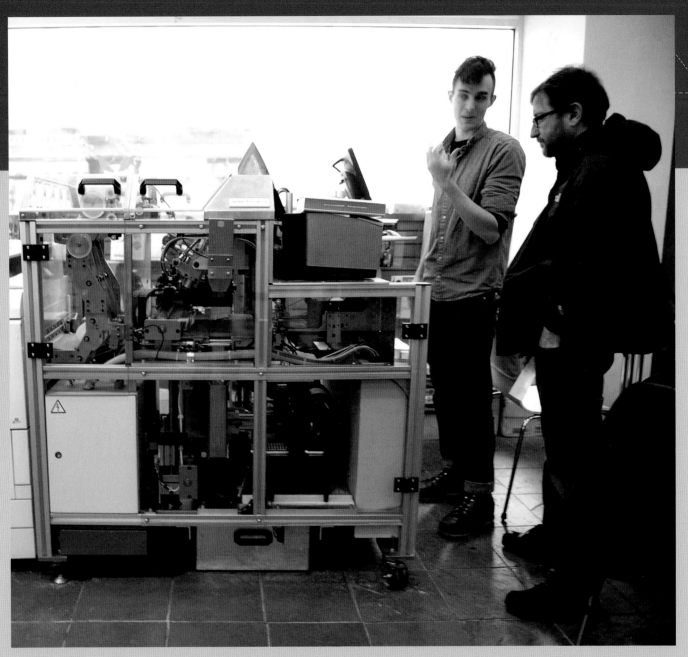

A customer watches as a book is printed on demand by an Espresso machine in a New York bookstore.

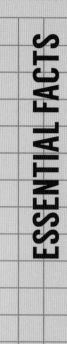

DATE OF INVENTION

1440s

KEY PLAYERS

- ▶ Pi Sheng, inventor of movable type, c. 1041 CE, China

- ▶ Johannes Gutenberg, inventor of the printing press with movable type, c. 1440s, Germany

- ▶ Johann Fust, Gutenberg's business partner and competitor

KEY TECHNOLOGIES

- ▶ Ink and paper suitable for printing

- ▶ A press system

- ▶ Movable type

EVOLUTION AND UPGRADES

- ▶ Steam-powered cylinder press, 1812

- ▶ Rotary printing press, 1847

- ▶ Offset printing, 1906

- ▶ Phototypesetting, c. 1946

- ▶ Computers and digital printing, 1960s–present

IMPACT ON SOCIETY

The printing press replaced laborious hand copying with a way to quickly make many exact copies of books and other materials. The spread of this technology allowed for more rapid dissemination of knowledge and ideas than ever before. Easy access to books increased education levels and dispersed scientific findings, political theories, and religious thought. The quick exchange of ideas contributed to scientific, religious, and political revolutions and set the stage for today's information-based society.

QUOTE

"Print proved the great engine for the spread of enlightened views and values."

—*Roy Porter*, The Creation of the Modern World

alloy

A mixture of two or more metals.

baseline

The line upon which letters "sit" in printed text.

cast

To form something, such as type, by pouring soft or molten metal into a mold.

cuneiform

A wedge-shaped writing system used by the people of ancient Mesopotamia.

engrave

To cut a design or text into a surface.

hieroglyphics

A system of writing used by ancient Egyptians, made up of pictures and symbols that stand for words.

indulgence

Payment made to the Catholic church to forgive a person's sin.

libel

Publishing a false statement that is damaging to a person's reputation.

literacy

The ability to read and write.

manuscript

A book or document written by hand, especially one made before the invention of printing.

matrix

A mold for casting a letter.

movable type

A system of printing that used movable pieces to reproduce the letters and other characters of a document.

parchment

A material to write on made from the skin of a sheep or goat.

patrician

An aristocrat or nobleman.

phonetic

Representing the sounds of speech with a set of symbols, each denoting a separate sound.

Reformation

A 1500s movement for the reform of abuses in the Roman Catholic Church ending in the establishment of the Protestant Church.

relic

An object that has religious significance.

scribe

A person who copies manuscripts and documents.

scroll

A roll of parchment or papyrus, used especially for writing documents.

vernacular

The ordinary spoken language of a country or region.

woodcut

A print made from a piece of carved wood.

ADDITIONAL RESOURCES

SELECTED BIBLIOGRAPHY

Eisenstein, Elizabeth L. *The Printing Press As an Agent of Change*. Cambridge, UK: Cambridge UP, 1979. Print.

Kilgour, Frederick G. *The Evolution of the Book*. New York: Oxford UP, 1998. Print.

Porter, Roy. *The Creation of the Modern World: The Untold Story of the British Enlightenment*. New York: Norton, 2000. Print.

Sonn, William. *Paradigms Lost: The Life and Deaths of the Printed Word*. Lanham, MD: Scarecrow, 2006. Print.

FURTHER READINGS

Bridgman, Roger. *1,000 Inventions and Discoveries*. New York: DK, 2014. Print.

Spangenburg, Ray, and Diane Kit Moser. *The Rise of Reason: 1700–1799*. New York: Facts on File, 2004. Print.

Vander Hook, Susan. *Johannes Gutenberg: Printing Press Innovator*. Minneapolis, MN: Abdo, 2009. Print.

WEBSITES

To learn more about Essential Library of Inventions, visit **booklinks.abdopublishing.com**. These links are routinely monitored and updated to provide the most current information available.

FOR MORE INFORMATION

For more information on this subject, contact or visit the following organizations:

The Museum of Printing

800 Massachusetts Avenue
North Andover, MA 01845
978-686-0450
http://www.museumofprinting.org

The Museum of Printing includes collections of printing equipment and records related to print history. A gallery features a timeline covering the 500-year history of the printing press.

Platen Press Museum

3053 Sheridan Road
Zion, IL 60099
847-731-1945
http://www.platenpressmuseum.com

This museum works to preserve historic printing techniques. Its collections include many varieties of printing presses and type.

SOURCE NOTES

Chapter 1. A World without Print

1. William Sonn. *Paradigms Lost: The Life and Deaths of the Printed Word.* Lanham, MD: Scarecrow, 2006. Print. 22.

2. Ibid.

3. "Lascaux Grotto." *Encyclopedia Britannica.* Encyclopedia Britannica, 2015. Web. 3 Mar. 2015.

4. "Burrap Peninsula Rock Art among World's Oldest." *AustralianGeographic.* NineMSN, 18 Apr. 2013. Web. 8 Oct. 2014.

5. Lucien Febrve and Henri-Jean Martin. *The Coming of the Book: The Impact of Printing, 1450–1800.* London: NLB, 1976. Print. 186.

6. "Google: 129 Million Different Books Have Been Published." *PCWorld.* IDG Consumer, 6 Aug. 2010. Web. 3 Mar. 2015.

Chapter 2. The Origins of Printing

1. "Cuneiform Tablets." *BAS Library.* Bible Archaeology Society, Mar./Apr. 2005. Web. 3 Mar. 2015.

2. William Sonn. *Paradigms Lost: The Life and Deaths of the Printed Word.* Lanham, MD: Scarecrow, 2006. Print. 18.

3. Heather Phillips. "The Great Library of Alexandria?" *Library Philosophy and Practice* 2010. Web. 3 Mar. 2015.

4. Ernest Satow. "Further Notes on Movable Types in Korea and Early Japanese Printed Books." *Transactions of the Asiatic Society of Japan.* Vol. 10. Yokohama, Japan: R. Meiklejohn, 1882. *Google Book Search.* Web. 3 Mar. 2015.

Chapter 3. The Man from Mainz

1. Gertrude Burford Rawlings. *The Story of Books*. London: Hodder and Stoughton, ca. 1901. *Project Gutenberg*. Web. 3 Mar. 2015.

2. "Gutenberg Bible Census." *Clausenbooks*. Clausen Books, 27 Nov. 2014. Web. 3 Mar. 2015.

3. "Making the Bible: The Vellum." *British Library: Gutenberg Bible*. British Library, n.d. Web. 3 Mar. 2015.

4. "Gutenberg Bible Fast Facts." *Harry Ransom Center*. University of Texas at Austin, n.d. Web. 3 Mar. 2015.

Chapter 4. How Gutenberg Did It

1. John Man. *Gutenberg: How One Man Remade the World with Words*. New York: Wiley, 2002. Print. 199.

Chapter 5. The Print Revolution

1. Lucien Febrve and Henri-Jean Martin. *The Coming of the Book: The Impact of Printing, 1450–1800*. London: NLB, 1976. Print. 182.

2. Ibid. 186.

3. Ibid. 249.

4. Ibid. 280.

Chapter 6. Early American Printing

1. "History of Newspapers." *Rag Linen Online Museum of Historic Newspapers*. Todd Andrlik and Rag Linen, 2015. Web. 3 Mar. 2015.

2. "Facts and Figures about the Newspaper Collection." *American Antiquarian Society*. American Antiquarian Society, n.d. Web. 3 Mar. 2015.

3. John T. Winterich. *Early American Books & Printing*. Detroit: Gale, 1974. Print. 91.

4. Jack Lynch. "Every Man Able to Read: Literacy in America." *Colonial Williamsburg Journal* Winter 2011. Web. 3 Mar. 2015.

Chapter 7. The Age of Reason

1. Roy Porter. *The Creation of the Modern World: The Untold Story of the British Enlightenment.* New York: Norton, 2000. Print. 91.

2. Ibid. 73.

3. Jeremy Black. "Newspapers and Politics in the 18th Century." *History Today* 36.10 (Oct. 1986). Web. 3 Mar. 2015.

4. Ibid.

5. Jean-Jacques Rousseau. *The Social Contract and Other Later Political Writings.* Victor Gourevitch, ed. Cambridge, UK: Cambridge UP, 1997. *Google Book Search.* 3 Mar. 2015.

6. "Encyclopédie." *Encyclopedia Britannica.* Encyclopedia Britannica, 2015. Web. 3 Mar. 2015.

7. "The Encyclopedia of Diderot and d'Alembert Collaborative Translation Project." *University of Michigan Library.* University of Michigan Library, n.d. Web. 3 Mar. 2015.

8. John R. Pannabecker. "Diderot, the Mechanical Arts and the *Encyclopédie.*" *Journal of Technology Education* 6.1 (Fall 1994). *Virginia Tech Digital Library and Archives.* Web. 3 Mar. 2015.

9. Junius P. Rodriguez. "Uncle Tom's Cabin." *Slavery in the United States: A Social, Political, and Historical Encyclopedia.* Vol. 1. Santa Barbara, CA: ABC-CLIO, 2007. *Google Book Search.* 3 Mar. 2015.

10. "Printing Yesterday and Today." *Harry Ransom Center.* University of Texas at Austin, n.d. Web. 3 Mar. 2015.

11. "Improving the Press: Stronger, Better, Faster." *Treasures of the MacDonald Collection.* Special Collections & Archives Research Center, Oregon State University Libraries, n.d. Web. 3 Mar. 2015.

Chapter 8. Technology Moves Forward

1. John Hendel. "Celebrating Linotype, 125 Years Since Its Debut." *Atlantic*. Atlantic Monthly Group, 20 May 2011. Web. 3 Mar. 2015.

2. Mergenthaler Linotype Company. "Weights and Measurements for Linotype Machines for Export." n.p., n.d. *Internet Archive*. Web. 3 Mar. 2015.

Chapter 9. The Digital Age

1. "Project Gutenberg." *Project Gutenberg*. Project Gutenberg, n.d. Web. 5 Mar. 2015.

2. Robert Darnton. "National Digital Library Project Is Launched." *New York Review of Books*. NYREV, 25 Apr. 2013. Web. 3 Mar. 2015.

3. "Unit Sales of the U.S. Book Market from 2010 to 2013 (in Billions)." *Statista: The Statistics Portal*. Statista, 2015. Web. 3 Mar. 2015.

4. Kathryn Zickuhr and Lee Rainie. "E-Reading Rises as Device Ownership Jumps." *Pew Research Center*. Pew Research Center, 16 Jan. 2014. Web. 5 Mar. 2015.

5. Mark Twain. "The Work of Gutenberg." *Hartford Daily Courant* 27 June 1900. *TwainQuotes.com*. Web. 3 Mar. 2015.

6. Claire Fallon. "Print Books Outsold E-Books in First Half of 2014." *HuffPost Books*. TheHuffingtonPost.com, 6 Oct. 2014. Web. 5 Mar. 2015.

7. "DiamondStar." *Mitsubishi Heavy Industries Europe*. Mitsubishi, 2015. Web. 5 Mar. 2015.

INDEX

alphabet, 19–20, 25
American colonies, 15, 55, 58–68, 72, 76
Aristotle, 20, 52

Barker, Robert, 51
Bay Psalm Book, 60
Beccaria, Cesare, 72
Bell, Robert, 67
Bible, 8, 26–27, 33, 35–36, 45, 51, 60
Blackstone, William, 76
block printing, 22–25, 52
Bradford, William, 61, 65

Campbell, John, 64
Carlson, Chester F., 89
casting, 24, 31, 35, 41–42, 43, 61, 82, 85, 86
Catholicon, 45
children's materials, 62, 67, 78
China, 15, 19, 22, 24–25, 26
clay tablets, 16, 18
clay type, 15, 24
codex, 24
Columbus, Christopher, 54
Common Sense, 67
computer, 15, 90, 92, 94, 96, 98
computer to film printing, 94
computer to plate printing, 94
Copernicus, 15, 53
copier, 15, 89, 92
Cosby, William, 65
cuneiform, 18
cylinder press, 15, 79, 80, 82, 84, 87

d'Alembert, Jean, 77
Day, Stephen, 60
Dead Sea Scrolls, 11
Declaration of Independence, 72, 94
Diderot, Denis, 77
Donatus, 33, 34
Dritzehn, Andreas, 31–32
Dunlap, John, 72

e-book, 94, 95–96, 97
education, 8, 13, 27, 48, 52–54, 67, 74, 76
Egypt, 8, 11, 15, 16, 18, 20
Encyclopédie, 77
England, 8, 9, 14, 15, 49, 51, 52, 58, 61, 62, 67–68, 72, 73–75, 79
engraving, 52, 53, 68, 84
Enlightenment, 70–76, 77

France, 9, 11, 14, 49, 52, 54, 75–76, 77, 84
Franklin, Ann, 62
Franklin, Benjamin, 62, 65–67, 76
Franklin, James, 65–66
Fust, Johan, 34–36

Germany, 6, 9, 11, 15, 28, 31, 33, 34, 36, 43, 48, 49, 51–52, 53, 72, 79, 80, 97
Glover, Elizabeth, 58
Google Books, 95
Great Library, 20
Greeks, 8, 19, 20, 48, 49, 52
Green, Anne Catherine, 62

Gutenberg, Johann, 6–8, 12–13, 15, 25, 26, 28–36, 38–45, 97
Gutenberg Bible, 35–36

Haas, Wilhelm, 78
Harris, Benjamin, 63, 64
Hart, Michael, 94
Heilmann, Andreas, 31, 33
hieroglyphics, 18
Hoe, Richard, 15, 82, 84

Indus River valley, 18–19
ink, 6, 8, 22, 24, 27, 38, 40, 43, 44–45, 52, 61, 79–80, 84, 87, 92
inkjet printing, 92
Intertype Fotosetter, 89

King James Bible, 51
Koenig, Friedrich, 15, 80, 82
Korea, 24–25

Lanston, Tolbert, 86
laser printing, 90, 92, 93
Latin, 8, 9, 11, 18, 20, 27, 33, 34, 40, 45, 49, 54, 74
Liberator, 78
Lindisfarne Gospels, 27
Linotype, 15, 85
Locke, John, 72, 75
Luther, Martin, 51–52

manuscript, 11, 19, 20–21, 26, 27, 35
Maryland Gazette, 62
Massachusetts Spy, 67
matrix, 40–42, 85–86

Mergenthaler, Ottmar, 15, 85
Mesopotamia, 15, 16, 18
Monotype, 85
Montesquieu, Baron de, 75, 77
movable type, 8, 15, 23–25, 42, 79

newspaper, 8, 48, 61, 63–66, 67, 68, 72, 73, 75, 78, 79, 98
Newton, Isaac, 73–74
Nicholson, William, 79
Nuthead, Dinah, 62, 64
Nuthead, William, 64

offset printing, 15, 87, 88, 94, 98
On the Fabric of the Human Body, 53–54
On the Revolution of Heavenly Spheres, 52–53

Paine, Thomas, 67–68
paper, 6, 8, 15, 22, 24, 25, 26, 35, 38, 41, 42, 43, 45, 48, 51, 52, 61, 67, 79, 80, 84, 87, 89, 92
papyrus, 18, 19–21, 22
parchment, 19, 20–21, 22, 26
Pennsylvania Gazette, 66
Pennsylvania Magazine, 67
Pennsylvania Packet, 72
photoengraving, 84–85, 87
phototypesetting, 87, 89
Pi Sheng, 15, 24
platen, 43–45, 79
Plato, 19–20
politics, 8, 18, 48, 54, 67, 76
Poor Richard's Almanack, 66
Prince, The, 54

print on demand, 98
Project Gutenberg, 94
propaganda, 68
Ptolemy Soter, 20
Publick Occurrences, 63

religion, 8, 11, 18, 24, 25, 26, 48, 51, 58, 62, 65, 70
Revere, Paul, 68
Riffe, Hans, 31, 33
Rittenhouse, William, 61
Romans, 8, 20, 27, 48, 52
Rosa, Pedro, 54
Rousseau, Jean-Jacques, 76, 77
Rubel, Ira W., 15, 87

Santángel, Luis de, 54
Saspach, Konrad, 31–32
Schoeffer, Peter, 35–36
science, 8, 48, 52–54, 67, 70, 73–74
Scotland, 51, 52, 73, 75, 76, 79
scribes, 9, 11, 13, 16, 18, 19, 22, 27, 35
Sejong, 25
Senefelder, Alois, 15, 79–80, 87
Sibylline Prophecies, The, 33
slavery, 77–78
Smith, Adam, 75
Stanhope, Charles, 79

Talbot, William Henry Fox, 84, 87
36-Line Bible, 45
Thomas, Isaiah, 67
Ts'ai Lun, 15, 22
Twain, Mark, 97

type case, 43
Type Revolving Machine, 82–84
typesetter, 43, 86

United States, 65, 70, 72, 78, 82, 85, 86, 87, 89, 97
universities, 9, 11, 27, 58, 73

Vattel, Emmerich de, 76
vernacular, 27, 49
Vesalius, Andreas, 15, 53
Voltaire, 76, 77

Washington, George, 76
web press, 84
Wei Tan, 22
Wilberforce, William, 78
Wollstonecraft, Mary, 73, 74
women, 62, 74
wooden-screw press, 43–45, 79

Xerox Corporation, 15, 89, 92

Zenger, John Peter, 65

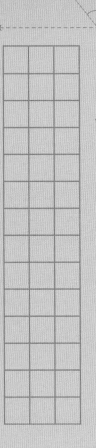

About the Author

Nel Yomtov is an award-winning author of nonfiction books and graphic novels for young readers. His writing passions include history, geography, military, nature, sports, biographies, and careers. Yomtov has also written, edited, and colored hundreds of Marvel comic books. Nel has served as editorial director of a children's nonfiction book publisher and as executive editor of Hammond World Atlas book division. Nel lives in the New York City area with his wife.